Mocha

Mocha

MICHAEL TURBACK
PHOTOGRAPHY BY LEO GONG

TEN SPEED PRESS
Berkeley | Toronto

Ten Speed Press
PO Box 7123
Berkeley CA 94707
www.tenspeed.com

Distributed in Australia by Simon and Schuster
Australia, in Canada by Ten Speed Press Canada,
in New Zealand by Southern Publishers Group,
in South Africa by Real Books, and in the United
Kingdom and Europe by Publishers Group UK.

Cover and text design by Betsy Stromberg
and Katy Brown
Food and props styled by Karen Shinto
Photo assistants Akiko Seki and Harumi Seki

Library of Congress Cataloging-in-
Publication Data
Turback, Michael.
  Mocha / Michael Turback ; photography by Leo
Gong.
     p. cm.
  Includes index.
  ISBN-13: 978-1-58008-861-9 (alk. paper)
  ISBN-10: 1-58008-861-9 (alk. paper)
 1. Cookery (Chocolate) 2. Cookery (Coffee) I.
Title. II. Title: Chocolate and coffee.
  TX767.C5T87 2007
  641.3'374—dc22

ISBN 13: 978-1-58008-861-9
ISBN 10: 1-58008-861-9

First printing, 2007
Printed in China

1 2 3 4 5 6 7 8 9 10 — 12 11 10 09 08

Contents

For Vic & Winnie

Acknowledgments

This book was written with the help of a great many people who contributed their energies to the project. I would like to start with a special acknowledgment for the support of my wife Juliet, who patiently put up with my late-night and weekend writing activities and who kept me excited about the project.

I was honored to have the blessing and guidance of Andrea Slitti, the celebrated Tuscan chocolatier and coffee roaster, a man who will tell you that the voluptuous combination of chocolate and coffee is why God invented eating.

My thanks go in full measure to the generous efforts and inventive recipes contributed by some of the planet's best chocolatiers, pastry chefs, and baristas. This book is a tribute to their passions.

Thanks, too, for wisdom and support from Fortune Elkins, Sherri Johns, Shelly Burgess, Britt Figueroa, Michael Szyliowicz, Brian Martell, Anil Rohira, Rogerio David, Peter O'Donnell, Barbara Lang, and, of course, very special thanks to Meryl Davis and Marjorie Rugg, my chief assistants in the preparation of this volume.

It has once again been a pleasure to work with the fabulously talented people at Ten Speed Press, in particular, Veronica Randall, my editor. I must extend a very special appreciation to Dennis Hayes, adventurer and friend. This book would not have been possible without his enthusiasm and energy.

Some of the material in this book was inspired by conversations, email, and advice from colleagues in the hospitality industry. I have credited these sources where known, but if I have overlooked anyone, please accept my apologies with my thanks.

Finally, I want to acknowledge the most important people in the life of this book—the readers. Thank you!

Chocolate & Coffee:

Although seemingly contradictory in their culinary natures, chocolate and coffee have more in common than they have differences. Both ingredients, derived from roasted beans grown in tropical and subtropical regions, are synonymous with sensory delight and noble thoughts, their incorporation into modern culture preceded by centuries of mythology and tradition.

Mature cacao trees produce pods the size of a human hand, and inside these fruits are the tree's seeds, known as cocoa beans to the trade. The less statuesque coffee tree produces berries the color and size of small cherries. Inside the skin and pulp are nestled twin coffee beans, flat sides facing each other.

Although worlds apart in origin and genealogy, chocolate and coffee eventually came to share some of the same geography. The coffee tree, native to Africa, was first cultivated in the Ethiopian province of Kaffa, giving the drink its name. By the eighteenth century, Jesuit missionaries from Spain and Portugal had transplanted African coffee into South America, where the volcanic soil of the Andes Mountains, along with mild temperatures and abundant rainfall, enabled the new crop to flourish. Today, Brazil and Columbia produce most of the planet's coffee.

The journey of chocolate was just the reverse. Native cacao from Mexico, Costa Rica, and Venezuela supplied Europe and the Americas with chocolate until the nineteenth century when the Dutch introduced New World cacao to the Gold Coast of West Africa. And today, as fate would have it, the African nations of Ghana and Nigeria have become the leading growers of cacao.

> The smell of hot chocolate on a cold day is a great temporary panacea for most any troubles.
>
> BRIAN LUKE SEAWARD,
> *THE ART OF CALM*

As with wine grapes, the totality of environment or *terroir* proves critical to the development of specific flavor notes within both cacao and coffee beans. A singular variety often dominates in each specific latitude and growing region, imparting an expected taste profile uniquely characteristic of those beans. Coffee beans from the rich volcanic soils in the highlands of Kenya are usually roasted lightly so their signature body, acidity, and blackcurrant flavors are preserved. Chuao, a small village in the northern coastal range of Venezuela, shielded by mountains from all but the warm Caribbean breezes, is home to distinctive, assertive cacao with undertones of exotic fruits and traces of vanilla.

While the blending of cacao beans, and the blending of coffee beans, are considered art forms, ensuring quality and consistency, there is steady movement toward single-origin chocolates and coffees, derived from only one type of bean from a specific locale. These unblended, appellation-specific products capture the pure essence of beans grown and harvested from a single farm or estate, much to the delight of sophisticated palates everywhere.

Throughout early coffee history, Arab traders held a monopoly on the exportation of the precious beans from the port of Mocha in southwestern Yemen on the Red Sea. At one time the name "mocha" was synonymous with coffee, yet the term has become somewhat ambiguous. On the palate, roasted native Mocha beans exhibit distinct chocolatey notes, and for that reason, legend persists, the same term is used to describe the marriage of coffee and chocolate.

> No coffee can be good in the mouth that does not first send a sweet offering of odour to the nostrils.
>
> HENRY WARD BEECHER

As sixteenth-century sailing ships carried goods from the Arabian Peninsula across the Mediterranean, the Italian port of Venice became coffee's gateway to European markets. Merchants in Venice and Turin opened the earliest coffee houses, and when Spanish drinking chocolate was first introduced to Turin, it was mixed with coffee and cream into a stimulating novelty called *bavareisa.*

In Italy, confectioners from the "Sweet Piemonte" region developed the art of combining these two culinary treasures, culminating with *bicerin* (meaning "small glass"). This short, rich chocolate and espresso beverage is still served in a clear glass so the drinker can admire the layers of dark liquids mingling together with each sip.

Outside Italy, caffè latte has become the basis for a drink of one-third espresso and two-thirds steamed milk. The ubiquitous caffè mocha, a latte with the addition of chocolate powder or chocolate syrup, only hints at the possibilities of more complex combinations.

Chocolate and coffee each run the gamut from light to dark, bitter to sweet, and, when blended together in creative drinks and desserts, bring an elegant sophistication to the table. The synergy of these two dependable pleasures is obvious at the finish of dinner, when they often combine to aid digestion and elevate the mood. On the affinity of the two ingredients, L'Academie de Cuisine pastry chef and chocolatier Anil Rohira observes: "Like a happy couple, chocolate and coffee bring out each other's best qualities."

The compatibility of chocolate and coffee is a fertile subject, in readiness for more exploration. To that end, I have been occupied in the agreeable task of collecting recipes—from practiced hands and curious palates, engaged in devious experiments to find new delights in the fusion of the two ingredients. As the assembled chocolatiers, pastry chefs, and baristas unite the flavors of chocolate and coffee so naturally and seamlessly, it reminds me that the world is still full of magic. It's nothing short of spellbinding when two things merge to form something entirely new without losing their individuality.

Chocolate and coffee, in my considered opinion, provide the most dazzling of all flavor combinations. For you, dear reader, I offer a book's worth of taste poems to prove it. May you enjoy many a convivial hour in putting them to the test.

Michael Turback
Ithaca, New York

Mochalogue:

Chocolate and coffee prove to be kindred companions in a range of drinks and desserts, and this book is intended to advance the current state of the art with contributions from an impressive multitude of professionals.

The theme uniting this assemblage has less to do with the individual ingredients than in how they come together in glorious, often unexpected ways. But first, let's take a few pages to discuss the essential elements in a little more depth.

INGREDIENTS

The essence of the chocolate-coffee partnership lies as much with an informed choice of ingredients as with an informed approach to preparation. While many of the items that follow are available at your local supermarket or coffee shop, I encourage you to stock your cupboard with supplies that may be more challenging to find.

Master chocolatiers and baristas are, each in their own way, as selective and fanatical about ingredients as vintners are about grape varieties. As mentioned earlier, cacao and coffee develop different characteristics when grown in different regions. Thus it follows that each region contributes a distinctive aroma, personality, and complexity to the preparation's final character.

Chocolate

A package of fine chocolate will list the percentage of cocoa butter and/or cacao solids it contains. High-quality chocolate contains more fat, which results in more flavor and a luxurious feeling on the tongue, or mouthfeel. The higher the number, the better the chocolate. Superior chocolates, the "couvertures" used by professional chefs, consist of 56 to 70 percent cacao solids and include 31 percent cacao butter.

> There is no metaphysics on earth like chocolate.
>
> FERNANDO PESSOA

Unsweetened chocolate is pure chocolate liquor and about 50 percent cocoa butter. Bittersweet chocolate blends at least 35 percent liquor with as much as 50 percent cocoa butter, sugar, and vanilla. Semisweet chocolate has the same ingredients as bittersweet with the addition of more sugar. Milk chocolate, which contains about 10 percent chocolate liquor, takes the process a step further by adding about 12 percent milk solids. Some of the recommended chocolates come in blocks and must be chopped or shaved before use.

The recipes in this book mostly call for dark, semisweet, or bittersweet chocolate and a few use white chocolate. (Because it does not contain cacao solids, white chocolate is technically not a chocolate.) Where it makes a difference, the exact percentage of cacao or specific maker is indicated.

A mocha-inspired preparation is meant to be a balance between the chocolate and the coffee. Base the selection of each chocolate for your recipe in combination, rather than separately. Chocolates often behave differently once they become part of a blend.

Cocoa Powder

Cocoa powder is made by extracting much of the cocoa butter richness from the chocolate liquor (ground, roasted cocoa beans), then pulverizing the dry residue into a fine, soft powder.

There are two types of cocoa: natural (nonalkalinized) and Dutch process (alkalinized). Natural cocoa powder (also called unsweetened) is simply untreated cocoa powder. Dutch process cocoa has been treated with an alkali to make the powder more soluble. Along the way, "dutching" gives the cocoa a deep mahogany color and an Oreo cookie flavor. The most popular American brands of cocoa powder contain about 7 percent cocoa butter, while specialty and European cocoa powders contain 12 to 24 percent cocoa butter. Recipes in this book call for pure cocoa powder, not cocoa mixes that include artificial flavors, nonfat dry milk, preservatives, soy lecithin, vanilla, and sugar.

Cocoa powder is often used aesthetically, as a light dusting to add pleasing color and aromatics to a drink or dessert presentation.

Coffee

While there are over twenty species of coffee plants, only two, *robusta* and *arabica,* account for the lion's share of commercial coffees.

> Science is, on the whole, an informal activity, a life of shirt sleeves and coffee served in beakers.
>
> GEORGE PORTER

Robusta beans have a woody, bitter taste and aroma, and they are usually relegated to mass-produced, pre-ground coffee blends and freeze-dried products. In Italian tradition, robustas are often included in espresso blends to boost *crema,* the alluring layer of tiny, smooth bubbles that trap precious aromatics.

Arabica varieties, descendents of the original Ethiopian coffee trees, are the best beans down here where mortals tread, appreciated for distinctive bouquet, sweet, wine-like tones, and superior acidity or "high notes." Beans from different origins are blended to make a coffee that is higher in quality than any of the ingredients individually, often to create a proprietary or signature blend. But the highest-quality arabica varieties usually stand alone as single-origin and estate coffees. For a match with chocolate, it's better to avoid very bitter coffees or any with a scorched flavor.

As beans are lightly roasted, they change to a buttery gold color and develop a very mild, nutty flavor. Further roasting adds more body, and the darkest or French roast produces savory, rich characters with satisfying bittersweet and smoky flavors.

The difference between coffee and espresso is simply the amount of water that dilutes the grounds. An invigorating shot of espresso has the least amount of water, and therefore has a stronger, more concentrated taste profile. Instant coffees or espressos have been dried into soluble powders or granules, which can be quickly dissolved in hot water for consumption or employed as ingredients in recipes.

Syrups

In Europe, flavored syrups are added to mineral waters to make "Italian sodas." On this side of the Atlantic they serve a dual purpose of flavoring and sweetening lattes and cappuccinos, an idea conceived by "Brandy" Brandenburger of General Foods and first promoted by Torani & Company of San Francisco. Flavored syrups are highly concentrated, but when used judiciously, they can give sweet little bursts of flavor to creative mochas.

Spices

Spices are among the earliest commodities to have circumnavigated the globe in trade. The practice of adding these powerful, lyrical, sensual aromatics to enhance the natural flavors of both chocolate and coffee can be traced back many centuries.

For best results, buy small quantities of ground spices and store them in tightly-closed containers in a cool, dark, and dry place for no longer than a year. Before using, sniff them. If the fragrance of a spice has dimmed, toss it out. Chances are, the flavor has weakened as well and will do nothing to improve your recipe. If you're using nonsoluble spices, place them in a tea ball or wrap them in cheesecloth before dropping them into liquid so you can easily fish them out later.

Store vanilla beans completely submerged in granulated sugar. This process preserves not only the moisture and freshness of the beans, but also creates an aromatic vanilla sugar that can be used for making cookies and other baked treats.

Sweeteners

Sugar is persistently valued, not only for the sweetening of drinks and desserts, but for adding volume, tenderness, and texture.

Granulated white, or table, sugar has medium-sized granules and is most often called for in recipes. When heated, granulated sugar takes on a toffee-like color and flavor.

Confectioners' sugar, which has been crushed mechanically (and generally mixed with a little starch to keep it from clumping), is favored for its dissolving properties, especially in iced chocolate drinks.

Brown sugar is simply white sugar with a bit of molasses to give it texture and color. Its color will depend on the amount of molasses added during processing. The darker the color, the stronger the taste, so use one that suits your taste preference. Substituting brown sugar for white will add notes of caramel and molasses.

Honey adds sweetness as well as flavor, however, you may need to experiment as some honey varieties tend to overwhelm the subtleties of other flavors. Because honey is sweeter than table sugar, you'll need less of it to please your palate. For more robust, bittersweet flavors, natural molasses is a one-to-one substitute for honey.

Conversions & Equivalents

FLUID MEASURES

10 milliliters (ml) = 2 teaspoons (t)

50 ml = 3 tablespoons (T)

100 ml = 3½ ounces

250 ml = 1 cup + 1 (T)

500 ml = 1 pint + 2 (T)

1 liter = 1 quart + 3 (T)

1 teaspoon = 5 ml

1 tablespoon = 15 ml

1 ounce = 30 ml

1 cup = 235 ml

1 quart = 950 ml

1 gallon = 3¾ liters

DRY MEASURES

10 grams = ⅓ ounce

50 grams = 1¾ ounces

100 grams = 3½ ounces

250 grams = 8¾ ounces

500 grams = 1 lb + 1½ ounces

½ ounce = 14 grams

1 ounce = 28 grams

¼ pound = 112 grams

½ pound = 224 grams

1 pound = 448 grams

TOOLS & TECHNIQUES

Measuring

When measuring chocolate or coffee, an ounce is measured in weight, not volume. Professionals use scales to measure dry ingredients for greater speed and accuracy. Digital and balance scales are preferred, since they can be recalibrated to maintain accuracy. Spring-loaded scales are not as precise.

For home cooks, there are inexpensive digital scales available that will hold up to eleven pounds, are accurate to within ¼ ounce, and convert between grams and ounces.

To properly measure, first weigh the container in which each ingredient will be placed. Set the zero indicator at the container's final weight. Then add the ingredients. In effect, you have ignored the weight of the container and only included the weight of the chocolate or coffee.

As for equipment, most recipes can be prepared with utensils you probably already have in your kitchen: measuring cups and spoons, a scale, a serrated knife, a pot or two, and a wooden spoon or wire whisk. Use a scoop for powder and a shot glass for syrups. Set aside a few bowls and/or a set of demitasse cups for serving.

Chopping, Shaving & Grinding

Most superior-quality chocolate comes in blocks and must therefore be either shaved on a coarse cheese grater or chopped into small chunks (about $1/4$ inch) with a knife.

To work with chocolate, have your block at room temperature. Cold chocolate is too hard to cut, and room-temperature chocolate will chop into pieces without splintering. Use a long serrated knife and score at the point you want the break to occur to a depth of about $1/8$ inch. Press the knife into the chocolate with firm steady pressure at several spots along the scored line, advancing the knife a little deeper into the bar at each spot.

Hold both the handle and the dull side of the blade, and chop into small pieces, as uniformly-sized as possible so they will melt evenly in the liquid. (If the pieces are different sizes the chocolate won't melt evenly, and you risk scorching some of the smaller pieces while waiting for the larger ones to melt.)

To shave chocolate in a food processor, chill the chocolate, bowl, and blade first, then pulse the chocolate to desired shavings. (Some manufacturers are making their chocolate available in small wafers or disks called "pistoles". Their slim, uniform size eliminates the need for chopping or shaving.)

Proper coffee grinding begins with a burr mill that produces more evenly sized particles than a blade grinder. Again, the more uniform the coffee particles the more even the extraction. Most models allow for a choice of grind calibrations, including French press (a coarse grind), drip (a medium grind), and espresso (a fine grind). When selecting a grinder, make sure it has the settings you require.

Melting, Cooking & Brewing

The favored method for cooking the chocolate component is as simple as melting small pieces of chocolate by stirring with hot milk in a nonreactive pan. Heat the milk over medium-low heat, and remove the pan from the heat just before it reaches the boiling point. Overheating milk destroys the flavor and texture.

Ladle out a portion of the milk over the chocolate. Stir with a wooden spoon until well combined and the mixture forms a smooth paste, or ganache, which is the base for the drink. Continue adding milk and gently stir until all the milk has been incorporated. Substituting a portion of heavy cream adds to the richness of the drink, while displacing all or part of the whole milk with low-fat milk or water allows more of the chocolate's complexity and subtle flavor notes to come through.

Let the chocolate cook in the milk while continuously stirring for a minute or two, then remove from heat, and allow the blended liquid to steep for ten minutes. This gives it time to develop its full range of flavors. Return to the heat and bring gently back to a simmer before serving.

To retain its full aroma, the chocolate should be kept *under* a boil, and, ideally, its temperature should not exceed 180 degrees F. To gauge accurately, an instant-read thermometer comes in handy. The right tools, and respect for your ingredients, help to ensure the best result.

Recipes that combine chocolate and coffee usually call for espresso or at least very strong coffee. The relatively inexpensive French press, or *cafetiére,* works by combining coarsely ground coffee beans with boiled water. The mixture is allowed to soak, then the grounds are pressed to the bottom of a glass cylinder, leaving behind filtered, rich coffee.

Brewing espresso is a culinary skill, and brewing great espresso at home requires a reliable machine. Thanks to its price and level of control, the semiautomatic has become the most common for home use. Its electric pump provides consistent pressure, forcing heated water through the finely ground coffee for thick, rich extraction.

Other than bean quality, duration of the brewing process is the single most important factor affecting the taste of espresso. With a semiautomatic machine, length of brewing time is controlled manually, a correctly extracted shot taking between 25 and 30 seconds.

Residue from the oils and grinds builds up with use and will affect the taste of your espresso. Take the time to clean the filter, water tank, and all other coffee tools regularly.

Mixing & Frothing

The more air you can get into a latte mixture, the frothier it will be. To impart a smooth, creamy texture to the drink: when the mixture begins to simmer, beat it vigorously with a wire whisk or fully submerge an immersion blender and whip until the surface of the drink is covered with foam. An elegant whisper of froth can be incorporated with a steam wand, the thin metal tube on an espresso machine connected to the boiler.

Frothing is easy with a bit of practice. Lower the wand into the milk (whole or 2 percent works best), injecting enough steam to create thousands of tiny micro-bubbles for a smooth and velvety texture.

Storing & Freshness

To store chocolate, wrap it well, first in foil and then in plastic, and keep it cool and dry at temperatures between 60 to 65 degrees F. Be sure to store it away from herbs, spices, and other aromatic foods, as chocolate picks up other flavors relatively easily.

Dark chocolate actually improves with age, like a fine wine, if stored under perfect conditions; it should be kept in a dark place or protected from light by wrapping paper. It is best not to refrigerate chocolate and it should never be frozen.

The whitish color that can rise to the surface on chocolate is called fat bloom. It means the cocoa butter has separated due to temperature fluctuation. While it's not a pretty sight, bloom does not affect taste, and the cocoa butter will be redistributed when the chocolate is melted.

Coffee beans begin to lose flavor if not stored under cool, dry conditions, protected from sunlight. Coffee is susceptible to damage from odors, temperature fluctuations, and moisture, and should be kept in an airtight container (not in refrigerator or freezer). If you must store coffee beans for a long period, separate portions into plastic bags, then wrap each bag tightly with aluminum foil.

It is ideal to buy coffee within no more than a few days of roasting. Grind your beans just before you're ready to brew.

Italian
Lessons

THE TREASURE OF TURIN

In this thriving northern Italian city, the blending of chocolate and coffee is a ritual, an enthusiasm, and in the case of *bicerin* (pronounced bee-chair-EEN), an obsession. Beginning with the Renaissance-era introduction of drinking chocolate to Turinese coffee houses, skillful local artisans nurtured the two ingredients into a variety of formulas and over time developed the epic drink named after the "little glass" in which it was, and is to this day, served.

This is not frivolous stuff. The pairing of ingredients in bicerin, despite its apparent simplicity, is an alliance of perfect proportions. With one part espresso, one part chocolate, and one part cream, it is a feat of culinary engineering. Each ingredient is poured carefully into a tempered glass, creating a composition of not only visually enchanting layers of liquids, but a sequence of vigorous taste sensations.

Each potent sip evokes the Caffé Al Bicerin, the beverage's namesake and most zealous keeper of history and tradition. Dating to 1763, this venerable confectionery in the bustling heart of Turin has welcomed the likes of Camillo di Cavour, Giacomo Puccini, Alexander Dumas, and Friedrich Nietzsche, all of whom enjoyed the fortifying properties of the dark, delicious restorative.

The ritual at Al Bicerin evolved in three versions: *pur-e-fior* (espresso and cream), *pur-e-barba* (espresso and chocolate), then finally the classic *un pô 'd tut* (espresso, chocolate, and cream). Because the world's sweetest, most prized hazelnuts cling to the hillsides that surround Turin, Gianduja (named for the comic puppet that stars in the city's annual carnivale), the toasted hazelnut-flavored chocolate, became as popular in the native bicerin as locally-roasted espresso. To faithfully connect with bicerin at home, your recipe should include Gianduja and a medium-dark roasted espresso in the true Italian tradition. The only thing that could possibly make the experience more pleasurable would be drinking it in Turin.

Bicerin Classico

Fortunato Nicotra, Felidia, New York, New York

Like most Italians, Fortunato Nicotra's passion for food began at an early age, and the rich environment of his childhood in Turin was the earliest influence for a career in the culinary arts. Today, this master chef attributes his culinary sensibilities to the legacy of his mother's cooking and his studies at the prestigious Institute Alberghiero.

Everyone drinks bicerin in his hometown, he explains, especially on winter mornings or during the *merende* (mid-afternoon) break. Children favor more chocolate than coffee in the formula, then graduate to a preference for equal proportions. "The drink is a meeting of two powerful ingredients," says the chef, "and neither is shy about its flavor." Since there is no better way to learn the art of bicerin than from a *discepolo della esperienza* (disciple of experience), Chef Nicotra graciously provides the most authentic recipe and proper technique.

6 ounces whole milk
3 ounces Gianduja or bittersweet chocolate, finely chopped or shaved
Pinch of salt
8 ounces espresso or very strong coffee
Whipped cream, lightly sweetened

To make the hot chocolate, heat the milk slowly in a small saucepan over low heat, stirring frequently, until steaming. Be careful not to scorch it. Add the chopped chocolate and salt to the steaming milk. Stir slowly over low heat. Do not allow the mixture to boil. Remove from the heat.

To assemble the bicerin, use 4 tempered short-stemmed glasses and pour 2 ounces of hot, freshly pulled espresso into each. Next, create a separate layer with 2 ounces of the warm chocolate on top of each espresso layer by pouring down the bottom of a tablespoon held against the side of the glass. Again using

CONTINUED

Bicerin Classico, *continued*

a tablespoon, pour another equal layer of cream over the top of each drink. The cream should be hand-whipped to a consistency just thick enough to float on top of the drink.

MAKES 4 SERVINGS

Friedrich Nietzsche, who said Turin was the one city he loved, said of it: "Tranquil, almost solemn. A classic landscape for the eyes and the feet . . . I'd never have believed that a city, thanks to its light, could become so beautiful!"

Bicerin Moderno

Caroline Yeh, Temper Chocolates, Boston, Massachusetts

The celebrated pastry chef from New York's Gotham Bar and Grill now indulges the lucky residents of Boston with artisan chocolates and handcrafted espressos in her shop, just off the lobby of the Commonwealth Hotel. Caroline Yeh recreates a respectful synthesis of past tradition yet forgoes fancy interpretation when she assembles the bicerin as a cold dessert shot, capturing the essential complexity of the original.

3 ounces dark chocolate, chopped

3 ounces whole milk

6 ounces espresso, chilled

4 ounces chilled heavy cream

Chocolate shavings or cocoa powder, for garnish

In a heavy saucepan, combine the dark chocolate with the whole milk and set over medium heat. Whisk until the chocolate is completely melted and remove from the heat. Set aside to cool. When the hot chocolate cools to room temperature, place in the refrigerator until completely cool.

To serve, place the chilled heavy cream into a cocktail shaker and shake vigorously for approximately 30 seconds, until the cream has thickened slightly.

Remove hot chocolate from the refrigerator and whisk. If the chocolate seems too thick, add a little cold milk to help thin it out. Pour approximately 3/4 ounce of the chilled hot chocolate into the bottom of a clear two-ounce shot glass. Then carefully pour 3/4 ounce of the chilled espresso on top of the hot chocolate, creating a layer of espresso. Finish each shot by pouring a layer of heavy cream on top of the espresso, to create a third layer. Garnish with a sprinkling of cocoa powder or chocolate shavings and serve immediately.

MAKES 2 TWO-OUNCE SHOTS

THE TUSCAN AESTHETIC

Monsummano Terme is a sleepy town in northern Tuscany, where some travelers come for the warm waters of the ancient grottos, others for the pleasures of chocolate and coffee at the Torrefazione di Caffè.

Opened as a roasting shop in 1969 by Luciano Slitti, a master at blending beans, the Torrefazione was transformed in 1988 into a *cioccolateria* by Slitti's son Andrea, who was enchanted by the combination of chocolate and coffee. In 1994, Andrea won the Grand Prix International de la Chocolaterie in Paris and is today considered a *maestro cioccolatiere*, one of the best chocolatiers in the world.

According to Andrea, "These chocolate and coffee drinks are a blend of energies immediately available for your body, as they match the charge of chocolate to the charge of coffee. They are excellent at breakfast time or ideal for regenerating after hard work or physical exertion."

Experience with and knowledge of chocolate and coffee provide a distinct advantage in determining a consummate blend of the two commodities. "Each has in itself the scent and taste of the other one," explains Andrea, "and if we put them together properly, the result is a great marriage!"

Andrea has determined which varieties of coffees make the best partners with chocolate. For example, Jamaica Blue Mountain coffee prepared as an infusion and blended with dark chocolate produces a graceful intensity; likewise, Kopi Luwak (from Sumatra) mixed with chocolate and cream is an "unforgettable experience." Andrea concludes that "one must combine chocolate with coffees whose characteristics include superior aromatics and exclude coffees that are high in acidity."

In the hands of this skilled and dedicated artisan, science and art merge, as chocolate and coffee are lovingly transformed into Bhaia-Mocca, Mokato, and Moretto.

Bhaia-Mocca

Andrea Slitti, Slitti Torrefazione, Monsummano Terme, Italy

1 ounce bittersweet chocolate, finely shaved

2 tablespoons boiling water

3 ounces espresso, Ethiopian blend

1/4 cup whipping cream

1/2 teaspoon coffee powder

3 coffee beans, whole

In a small bowl, combine the chocolate shavings with boiling water and stir until smooth. Pour into a terracotta cup. Add the espresso. In a medium bowl, whip the cream until thick but not yet holding stiff peaks. Spoon the whipped cream over the top. Lightly sprinkle with coffee powder and decorate with coffee beans.

MAKES 1 SERVING

Mokato

Andrea Slitti, Slitti Torrefazione, Monsummano Terme, Italy

1 ounce bittersweet chocolate, finely shaved

2 tablespoons boiling water

3 ounces espresso

$1/2$ teaspoon hazelnut paste

$1/4$ cup whipping cream

Brown sugar

In a small bowl, combine the chocolate shavings with boiling water and stir into a smooth liquid. Pour into a glass or cup. Pour in espresso, add hazelnut paste, and stir. In a medium bowl, whip the cream until thick but not yet holding stiff peaks. Spoon the whipped cream over the top. Lightly sprinkle with brown sugar.

MAKES 1 SERVING

Moretto

Andrea Slitti, Slitti Torrefazione, Monsummano Terme, Italy

2 ounces bittersweet chocolate, finely shaved

4 tablespoons boiling water

3 ounces espresso

1/4 cup whipping cream

Cocoa powder

In a small bowl, combine the chocolate shavings with boiling water and stir into a smooth liquid. Pour into a glass or cup. Add the espresso and stir until combined. In a medium bowl, whip the cream until thick but not yet holding peaks. Spoon the whipped cream over the top. Lightly sprinkle with cocoa powder.

MAKES 1 SERVING

Voltaire, the French Enlightenment deist and philosopher, was a prolific writer who produced works in almost every literary form, authoring plays, poetry, novels, essays, historical and scientific works, pamphlets, and over twenty thousand letters. At the restaurant La Procope in Paris, Voltaire reportedly drank as many as forty cups of his favorite mixture of coffee and chocolate every day.

Drinks

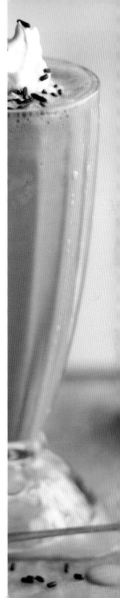

Triple Chocolate Maple Passion

Stuart Ross, Bull Dog Coffee, Toronto, Canada

"I want to make your tongue dance," says Stuart Ross of his creatively choreographed signature drink. Using an espresso blend with dark chocolate notes on the finish, this poetic transition of flavors and tones speaks soothingly and fluently, easing you throughout the length of the drink, one layer at a time. Taste the sweetness of the maple-infused cream, then drift down to the espresso and cream, and enjoy the kick of chili on your tongue. Go deeper still to taste the cream, espresso, and chocolate together, and surrender to the stream of sensations. Decide if you want to spoon it, sip it or, mix and sip. Your choice.

1 cup heavy cream

4 tablespoons maple syrup

1 tablespoon Guittard Dark Chocolate Syrup

1 ounce espresso

Pinch of chili powder

Mexican chocolate, shaved, for garnish

In a small mixing bowl, whip the heavy cream until slightly thickened. Add the maple syrup and continue whipping until the cream begins to hold its shape as soft peaks. Cover tightly with plastic wrap and reserve in refrigerator.

Drizzle the chocolate syrup down the inside of a demitasse cup. Add the espresso shot, then lightly dust the top of the espresso with chili powder. Spoon the maple syrup-infused whipped cream on top and garnish with shaved Mexican chocolate.

MAKES 1 SERVING

Café de Olla con Jarabe de Chocolate Mexicano

Barbara Sibley, La Palapa, New York, New York

It has been said that "cuisine is culture," and, without question, the richness of Mexican cuisine flows from the infusion of many cultures.

As a tribute to the sensibilities of her native Mexico, restaurateur Barbara Sibley has created a menu that celebrates her multicultural nation. Café de Olla reinterprets a traditional recipe for a smoky combination of sweetened black coffee with cinnamon-infused Mexican chocolate and other spices, prepared in traditional pots called *ollas*. "It's euphoric—so aromatic and full of memories," says Barbara, "The layers of coffee marry with chocolate for a warming, intoxicating, doubly Mexican brew."

CHOCOLATE SYRUP

1/2 cup water

1 Mexican chocolate tablet (approximately 2 ounces), coarsely chopped

5 cups water

4 ounces raw sugar or *piloncillo* (Mexican brown sugar)

1 1/2 sticks *canelle* or cinnamon

5 whole cloves

1/4 orange peel

1/2 cup dark roast coffee

6 teaspoons chocolate syrup

To make the chocolate syrup, in a small saucepan heat the water and add the chocolate, stirring continuously until the chocolate has melted and the liquid has thickened slightly. Do not boil or scorch. This syrup will keep for one week at room temperature or three weeks in the refrigerator. Alternatively it may be refrigerated and then allowed to come to room temperature 30 minutes before serving.

To assemble the café de olla, combine the water, sugar, cinnamon, cloves, and orange peel in a medium saucepan. Over medium-high heat, bring to a boil, stirring frequently to dissolve the sugar. Once it reaches a boil, remove from the heat and add the coffee. Cover and allow to steep for 10 minutes. Strain the mixture through a coffee filter fitted into a fine mesh sieve.

Pour the coffee into earthenware mugs and add a teaspoon of the chocolate syrup to each mug. Stir to combine and serve hot.

MAKES 6 SERVINGS

Each person has to discover what will set off those explosions in order to live, since the combustion that occurs when one of them is what nourishes the soul. That fire, in short, is its food.

LAURA ESQUIVEL, *COMO AGUA PARA CHOCOLATE* (*LIKE WATER FOR CHOCOLATE*)

Night in Casablanca

Michelle Myers, Boule Pâtisserie, Sona Restaurant, Los Angeles, California

Intriguingly sensual, dark, and brooding, Turkish coffee was first prepared during the sixteenth century, brewed in little pots called *ibriks*. From the markets in North Africa it spread throughout the Middle East and then to Europe and Russia. Michelle Myers intoxicates the palate with a rich chocolate-coffee union and cardamom-scented marshmallows. "This is my version of what I have always considered to be romantic Turkish coffee," she explains, "not the kind of coffee you grab on the way to work, but a drink for quiet enjoying." To finish, she suggests, brulée the marshmallows for extra caramelized gooeyness.

WHITE CARDAMOM MARSHMALLOW

1/2 cup confectioners' sugar

1/4 cup cornstarch

2 tablespoons butter, softened

3 tablespoons powdered gelatin

3/4 cup cool water

2 cups sugar

2/3 cups corn syrup

1/4 cup water

Pinch of salt

1 lemon, juiced and seeded

1/2 vanilla bean, seeds only (save the other half for the mocha)

1 teaspoon white cardamom, finely ground

MOCHA

1 cup whole milk

1 ounce water

2 tablespoons superfine sugar

2 ounces dark chocolate (72% cacao or higher), finely chopped

2 tablespoons Valrhona Dark Cocoa Powder

1/2 vanilla bean

Dash of ground clove

Single or double shot of espresso (depending on how strong you like it)

White cardamom marshmallow, for garnish

To make the white cardamom marshmallows, in a small bowl, mix the confectioners' sugar and cornstarch. Butter a 9 × 9-inch baking pan and sprinkle with the sugar and cornstarch mixture. In a mixing bowl, sprinkle the gelatin powder evenly over the cool water. (If the liquid is warm or hot, the gelatin cannot soften properly. Scattering the gelatin over the liquid's surface prevents the formation of lumps. As the gelatin absorbs the liquid, each granule becomes enlarged; this is known as blooming.) In a medium saucepan over medium-high heat, combine the sugar, corn syrup, and water. Bring to a boil until a candy thermometer reads 230°F. Pour the sugar mixture over the bloomed gelatin. Mix on medium speed for 5 minutes. Add salt and lemon juice. As the mixture turns opaque, white, and

fluffy, increase the speed to high. Add the vanilla bean seeds and cardamom. Whisk to combine. Spread the marshmallow into the buttered pan. When the marshmallow is set, cut into 1-inch squares.

When the marshmallows are ready to serve, in a small saucepan over medium-high heat, bring the milk and water to a boil. Whisk in the superfine sugar, the chocolate and cocoa powder, and the clove, return to a boil, and continue whisking until mixture has thickened. Add the espresso. Using an immersion blender, froth the mixture. Garnish with marshmallows and reserved vanilla bean and serve immediately.

MAKES 2 SERVINGS

Black-and-White Espresso Milkshake

Neil Kleinberg, Clinton Street Baking Company, New York, New York

At his Lower East Side outpost, Neil Kleinberg prepares a milkshake with the same care and attention that he uses when crafting an entrée. "Ice cream is to a milkshake as stock is to a soup," explains the chef. "Always start with a quality base." Neil starts with fresh, locally made ice creams (from Mark Thompson's Brooklyn Ice Cream Factory), then whirls in house-made fudge, espresso, and just enough milk to achieve the desired consistency. Balanced portions and correct techniques transform a good shake into a memorable one.

HOT FUDGE SAUCE

15 ounces Callebaut Semisweet Chocolate, finely chopped

1 1/2 cups Valrhona Cocoa Powder, sifted

1 cup light corn syrup

1/2 cup sugar

1/2 cup water

1/2 cup heavy cream

Pinch of salt

2 ounces butter

1/2 tablespoon vanilla extract

MILKSHAKE

3 ounces vanilla ice cream

3 ounces chocolate ice cream

2 tablespoons hot fudge

1 1/2 ounces espresso

Splash whole milk

Whipped cream, for garnish

Chocolate sprinkles, for garnish

CONTINUED

To make the hot fudge sauce, in the top of a double boiler, melt the chocolate and whisk in the cocoa powder. Set aside. In a small saucepan over medium heat, simmer the corn syrup, sugar, water, cream, and salt for about 4 minutes. Remove from heat. Whisk in the butter and vanilla. Slowly whisk in the chocolate mixture. Chill and reserve.

To make the milkshake, place the ice cream, hot fudge, espresso, and milk in a blender. Pulse for 2 minutes or until desired thickness is reached. Pour into tall glasses and top with whipped cream and sprinkles.

MAKES 2 SERVINGS

You are the one, divine coffee, whose sweet liquor, without altering the mind, can make the heart bloom.

ABBÉ DELILLE

Biochemically, love is just like eating large amounts of chocolate.

JOHN MILTON,
THE DEVIL'S ADVOCATE

La Mocha Loca

Laurie Beck, Monkey Love Dessert Bar, Pooler, Georgia

The possibilities of mochas are ever-expanding and embracing new flavors and ingredients. So before you toss out your next empty banana peel, perhaps you should consider unlocking its hidden flavorings. "Cooking intensifies the flavor of the peel," explains Laurie Beck of Monkey Love, "and adds an exotic note to the blend of chocolate, coffee, and hint of coconut." This curiously compelling drink is a showcase for ingredients that so generously bless mankind throughout the tropics. Note: Cream of coconut is available in most Asian foods and specialty grocery stores.

1 ounce Torani Italian Syrup (chocolate flavor)

3 ounces Coco López cream of coconut

3 ounces half-and-half

Banana peel

4 ounces espresso

Whipped cream, for garnish

Chocolate curls or cocoa powder, for garnish

Divide the Torani syrup into 2 mugs. In a steaming pitcher, gently steam the cream of coconut and half-and-half. Thoroughly clean the banana peel of all of its strings, then place in the hot cream and allow to steep for 2 minutes. Remove the peel from the cream and discard. Pour hot espresso over the chocolate syrup in each mug, then add the hot cream and stir gently. Top with whipped cream and chocolate curls or cocoa powder.

MAKES 2 SERVINGS

Caffé Borgia

Aaron Duckworth, Espresso Dell'Anatra, Kansas City, Missouri

From the powerful and influential Borgia family of Renaissance Italy came eleven cardinals, three popes, one queen, one saint—and the name for the beloved *caffé con cioccolato*. For his interpretation, Aaron "Duck" Duckworth, barista extraordinaire, amplifies the bright citrus notes of his espresso with orange syrup and completes the hat trick with dark chocolate from his Kansas City neighbor, Christopher Elbow. Several commercial orange-flavored syrups are available; Duck's choice is Robert Lambert's Blood Orange Syrup.

$1/2$ ounce orange-flavored Italian-style syrup

$1/2$ ounce Christopher Elbow's Chocolate Noir Dark Powder, plus a little extra for garnish

2 ounces espresso

6 ounces whole milk

Blood orange wedge, for garnish

In a preheated mug, combine the orange syrup and the chocolate powder. Pour the espresso over the chocolate, and stir to combine. Gently steam the milk, pour over the espresso, and stir to combine. Garnish with the blood orange wedge and dust with Christopher Elbow's Chocolate Noir Dark Powder.

MAKES 1 SERVING

Equatorial Trilogy

Joanne Mogridge, Cocoa West Chocolatier, Bowen Island, British Columbia, Canada

Vanilla beans contribute sweet, creamy notes and anise-like aromatics in this inspired preparation from chocolatier Joanne Mogridge. She uses freshly pulled espresso to liberate the vanilla's elegant flavors from the tiny "caviar" seeds inside each bean. Like chocolate and coffee, vanilla is an expression of its *terroir*, and Joanne suggests using long, slender Bourbon beans with rich taste, dark, oily skin, and an abundance of seeds.

6 tablespoons dark chocolate, finely chopped
2 whole Madagascar Bourbon vanilla beans
4 cups 2% milk
4 ounces espresso, dark roast
Chocolate shaving, for garnish

Divide the chopped chocolate among four tall mugs. Split the vanilla beans lengthwise, then cut them in half crosswise. Stand one piece of the bean in each mug, like a straw. Steam the milk. Pour a shot of espresso down the sliced vanilla bean. Stir gently to blend. Repeat for each serving. Pour the steamed milk down the vanilla bean. Top up each serving with the milk foam and chocolate shavings.

MAKES 4 SERVINGS

Caffé Shakerato con Cioccolato

Clay Gordon, New World Chocolate Society, Larchmont, New York

Agitation is the essence of this popular Italian coffee bar specialty. The drink takes shape when freshly pulled shots of espresso and chocolate syrup are combined with cracked ice and a bit of sugar in a cocktail shaker. It's shaken vigorously to aerate the espresso, then strained into a slim cocktail flute. At its best, the shakerato retains both chocolate richness and espresso complexity, layered with an attractive head of reconstituted crema. Clay Gordon recommends chilling the glasses in advance and using prepared simple syrup (equal parts sugar and water, boiled and cooled) rather than granulated sugar as the syrup dissolves more quickly in the cold liquid.

1 ounce espresso, room temperature

1 teaspoon simple syrup (see instructions at left)

A few drops of vanilla extract

1 1/2 ounces chocolate syrup

Twist of lemon or orange peel, for garnish

Fill a cocktail shaker halfway with cracked ice cubes. Pour the espresso, sugar syrup, and vanilla over the ice. Shake vigorously for at least 30 seconds and strain into a chilled glass that has been lined with a spiral of the chocolate syrup. Garnish with citrus peel.

MAKES 1 SERVING

Espresso Limon

Matt Riddle, Intelligentsia Coffee & Tea, Chicago, Illinois

"Simplicity is the ultimate sophistication," wrote Leonardo Da Vinci, an idea embraced by a member of the third wave of baristas—those dedicated coffeehouse professionals who raise their vocation to the level of sommelier. For this fusion drink, Matt Riddle employs dark, bittersweet chocolate from hometown Vosges Haut-Chocolat and lively citrus aromatics to exaggerate the subtle chocolate notes and fruit undertones in this rich, full-bodied espresso. Not only are the complementary flavors in perfect balance, the scented cream gives this charmer a palate-cleansing aftertaste.

6 ounces heavy whipping cream
1 tablespoon lemon zest
$1/2$ ounce dark chocolate, grated
2 ounces espresso
Fresh mint leaves, for garnish

To serve hot: Combine the whipping cream and lemon zest in a chilled cocktail shaker. Shake vigorously to infuse the zest with the cream and give it some extra body. Place $1/4$ ounce chocolate into each of two demitasse cups. Pour one shot of espresso into each cup. Stir lightly to combine. Pour 2 ounces of the whipped cream mixture into each glass. Garnish with mint leaves and serve.

To serve cold: Combine the whipping cream and zest as above. In another shaker, combine the chocolate and hot espresso. Stir to melt the chocolate. When the chocolate has completely melted, add 4 ice cubes and swirl to chill. Pour into glasses and top with the whipped cream mixture. Garnish and serve.

MAKES 2 SERVINGS

Sweetness

Bronwen Serna, Hines Public Market Coffee, Seattle, Washington

It can properly be called a small wonder, this simple yet satisfying drink created by one of the country's most accomplished baristas. "Sweetness" is Bronwen Serna's twist on traditional macchiato (usually an espresso with a dollop of foamed milk), enhanced with dark chocolate and sweetened with honey. The rich Valrhona powder melts easily and adds complementary notes to the nutty aftertaste of the espresso. After trying dozens of varieties, she settled on local clover honey to add depth and sweetness to the blend.

1 teaspoon Snoqualmie Valley Clover Honey

1 1/2 ounces espresso

1 teaspoon Valrhona Unsweetened Dark Chocolate Powder

1 ounce half-and-half

Preheat a 4-ounce espresso cup (with a spoon in the cup) with hot water. Add the honey, then pour the espresso over the honey. Combine the half-and-half and chocolate powder, gently steam, and then stir into the sweetened espresso.

MAKES 1 SERVING

Happiness. Simple as a glass of chocolate or tortuous as the heart. Bitter. Sweet. Alive.

JOANNE HARRIS

A cup of coffee is a call to action, the lubricant of great thoughts, conversation, and celebration.

THERESA FRANCIS-CHEUNG,
COFFEE WISDOM

Symphony in C

Andy Newborn, Barefoot Coffee Roasters, San Jose, California

At Barefoot, a café and roastery in the heart of Silicon Valley, the coffee is strong and rich, and the baristas are passionate and creative. Andy Newborn's version of cappuccino (or white espresso) is a symphony of sensory experiences: visual presentation, seductive aromas, velvety texture. It's a simple yet elegant improvisation, like an unsweetened mocha with about one-third the chocolate. He integrates raw organic cacao powder with espresso and trusts the deep chocolate flavor to hold its own in the mix. The "trick," he explains, "is to steam all the ingredients together—it adds a very pleasant lightness and flavor nuance to the drink."

2 ounces espresso

2 ounces half-and-half

1/2 teaspoon raw cacao powder

Pull espresso shots into a small steaming pitcher. Add the half-and-half and cacao powder. Lightly steam to 135 degrees F, which is a bit cooler than usual as this is a quick drink and is best slightly cooler. Make sure to invigorate the liquid without adding too much air to the mixture.

MAKES 1 SERVING

Ceremony

Anthony Ferguson, Cacao Anasa Chocolates, San Francisco, California

For centuries, as Arab and Persian merchants traded in African cacao, coffee, and spices, they gradually settled in eastern coastal towns and intermarried with local Africans and evolved as a distinct culture of Swahili, or coastal dwellers. In the Swahili language, *anasa,* the word for comfort, was the inspiration for Anthony Ferguson's chocolate enterprise. The historic East African *guhwah,* or coffee ceremony, is the basis for this recipe that adds the dimension of chocolate to native coffee spiced with cloves and black peppercorns. To recreate the exotic and relaxing atmosphere of an authentic "coffee ceremony," place an incense burner filled with sandalwood in the room where you are serving your guests.

1/4 cup coffee beans, whole

6 whole cloves

3 whole black peppercorns

2 cups water

6 ounces bittersweet or semisweet chocolate, coarsely chopped

1 1/2 cups whole milk

Preheat oven to 350 degrees F. Grind the coffee, cloves, and black peppercorns in a coffee or spice grinder. Spread the ground coffee and spices in a small sheet pan and toast for 5 minutes. Brew the coffee blend with 2 cups of water. Place the chocolate in a small saucepan. Pour 1 cup of the brewed coffee over the chocolate and stir until the chocolate is completely melted and smooth. Stir in the second cup of coffee and the milk. Set over medium heat and whisk continuously until the mixture just reaches a slow simmer. Do not allow the mixture to boil. Serve immediately or set aside and reheat just before serving.

MAKES 6 SERVINGS

Gulf Coast

Seneca Klassen, Bittersweet Café, Oakland, California

In 1806, when Napoleon's "Continental Blockade" of British goods resulted in a coffee shortage, the French began adding roasted chicory root to extend whatever coffee they still had. They delighted in the sweeter, richer taste of the coffee-chicory blend and continued to make coffee this way even when coffee was plentiful again. The practice persisted as French colonialists immigrated to New Orleans and the Gulf Coast. Chicory is a natural flavor enhancer, and its slight sweetness and caramel-like undertone enhance the blend of coffee and chocolate, resulting in a brew of deeper color, extra smoothness, and added body.

6 tablespoons ground coffee

2 tablespoons roasted chicory

1/2 cup Michel Cluizel Chocolate (85% cacao), shaved

1 tablespoon Valrhona Cocoa Powder

2 tablespoons sweetened condensed milk

1 cup water

1 cup milk

Cinnamon, ground, for garnish

Whipped cream, for garnish

In a small bowl, thoroughly combine all the dry ingredients. Pour the dry ingredients into the French press and top with sweetened condensed milk. Bring the water to a boil. Gently steam the milk. Add the water and milk to the French press and stir briskly with a spoon until all the ingredients are well blended. Allow the mixture to steep for 3 minutes. Slowly depress the screen on the French press until all the solids are collected and isolated at the bottom. Serve in a mug and top with cinnamon and whipped cream.

MAKES 2 SERVINGS

Mokka Peppar

Jonathan Rubenstein, Joe (the Art of Coffee), New York, New York

Be prepared for flavorful fireworks in this concoction from New York City's highly regarded coffeehouse, Joe (the Art of Coffee). Working with Chris Barnes, one of his dedicated baristas, Jonathan Rubenstein complicates his blend of cocoa and espresso with an ensemble of energetic peppers. You could call it "mocha with an attitude." The drink evokes early Arab traders who bewitched their coffee with generous additions of warming spices. To ensure optimum aromatics and flavor, buy whole peppercorns and crack them yourself in a mill just before adding to the recipe.

COCOA BASE

6 tablespoon Valrhona Cocoa Powder

1/4 cup sugar

1 teaspoon mild paprika

1/2 teaspoon cayenne

1/2 teaspoon Tellicherry black peppercorns, cracked

1/2 teaspoon pink peppercorns, cracked

1/2 cup water

WHIPPED CREAM

8 ounces heavy cream

2 tablespoons confectioners' sugar

1/2 teaspoon black peppercorns, cracked

1/2 teaspoon pink peppercorns, cracked

MOKKA PEPPAR

6 tablespoons cocoa base

6 ounces espresso

1/2 cup whole milk

1/2 cup half-and-half

1 ounce whipped cream

Valrhona Noir Dark Chocolate (64% cacao), shaved, for garnish

Pink peppercorns and Black peppercorns, cracked, for garnish

To make the cocoa base, combine the cocoa powder, sugar, paprika, cayenne, and peppercorns in a small bowl. In a small saucepan over medium-high heat, bring the water to a boil. Pour the water over the dry ingredients and whisk thoroughly. Set aside.

To make the whipped cream, in a medium bowl, whip the heavy cream and confectioners' sugar until peaks form. Fold in the peppercorns with a spatula until well incorporated. Refrigerate and set aside.

To assemble, place 1 tablespoon of cocoa base in each cup. Pour 1 ounce hot espresso over the cocoa base and stir to incorporate the espresso with the hot cocoa mixture. Steam the milk and half-and-half together. Pour 1 ounce of the steamed milk into each cup and add a $1/4$-inch of foam on top. Add a dollop of whipped cream and garnish with dark chocolate shavings and cracked pepper. Serve hot.

MAKES 6 SERVINGS

Life is good when you get to immerse yourself in the olfactory experience of chocolate and coffee.

DANA DAVENPORT, DILETTANTE CHOCOLATES

Coffee & Cardamom-Scented Hot Chocolate

Jenn Stone, JS Bon Bons, Toronto, Canada

Roasted beans from the African highlands of Kenya produce coffees with delightful complexity—lush and bright with fruity acidity, full body, and rich fragrance. Sometimes described as the "red wine" of coffees, its aromatics pair with chocolate in much the same way red wine compliments chocolate. The coffee bouquet mingles with sweetly piquant cardamom to magnify a classic hot chocolate made from Valrhona Palmira, crafted exclusively from Venezuelan Criollo beans—the chocolate equivalent of a single-estate vintage.

2 ounces whole Kenyan coffee beans

3 1/2 tablespoons cream

1 teaspoon freshly ground cardamom

3 tablespoons unsalted butter

9 ounces Valrhona Palmira Chocolate, finely chopped

12 ounces 2% milk

Whipped cream, for garnish

Ground cardamom, for garnish

To make the coffee infusion, combine the whole coffee beans and cream in a medium saucepan over medium-low heat. Bring to a simmer. Add the ground cardamom and remove from heat. Let steep approximately 2 hours until the cream has fully absorbed the coffee and cardamom flavors. Return to the heat and bring to a boil. Add the butter and stir to combine. Place chocolate in a stainless steel bowl and pour the cream mixture through a strainer directly onto the chocolate. Let sit for one minute and then stir until combined and completely smooth.

To make the hot chocolate, bring the milk to a boil in a medium saucepan over medium-high heat. Pour 2 ounces hot milk over 2 ounces of the coffee infusion for each serving. Stir each until smooth. Serve with whipped cream and a sprinkle of ground cardamom.

MAKES 6 SERVINGS

Mayan Mocha

David Blaine, Latah Bistro, Spokane, Washington

The idea of combining sweet and heat has been around since the Mayans first stirred honey and chiles into their chocolate potations. "Chocolate and coffee in raw form only hint at what they can do together," says Chef David Blaine, who combines ancient Mayan ingredients with modern Hispanic influences, including cinnamon, nutmeg, and cream, for a rich, full flavor and an intoxicating aroma. He chooses an espresso with hints of caramel and chocolate to reinforce flavors and temper the sweetness in a drink that becomes an anthropological study in a cup.

2 tablespoons Guittard Sweet Ground Chocolate

1 teaspoon ground cinnamon

$1/8$ teaspoon ancho chili powder

Pinch of freshly grated nutmeg

1 tablespoon honey

8 ounces of half-and-half

2 ounces espresso

In a large mug, add the chocolate, cinnamon, chili powder, nutmeg, and honey. Gently steam the half-and-half and pour over the chocolate-spice mixture. Stir to combine. Add the espresso and stir to combine.

MAKES 1 SERVING

Dirty Mocha

Christopher Elbow, Christopher Elbow Chocolates, Kansas City, Missouri

Like most creative chocolatiers, Christopher Elbow likes to revisit classic formulas. In a profession of artists, he is a master who marries ingredients and coaxes flavors from them in a way that suggests painterly eloquence, inspiring a cult of devotees in the process. His meditation on the mocha latté is dramatized by contrasting the color and flavor tonalities of dark and white chocolates. When stirred gently, the delightful complexity of the two chocolates spreads throughout the coffee. "Since this is an espresso-based drink," he explains, "the best espresso will provide the best results. Use your favorite brand."

DIRTY SYRUP

1/2 cup corn syrup

1/4 cup water

1 vanilla bean, split and scraped

2 ounces dark chocolate (70% cacao), coarsely chopped

2 ounces El Rey Icoa White Chocolate, coarsely chopped

MOCHA

1 ounce espresso

6 ounces 2% milk

2 tablespoons dirty syrup

Whipped cream, for garnish

To make the dirty syrup, in a medium saucepan, bring the corn syrup, water, and vanilla bean seeds to a boil. Remove from heat and whisk in the chocolate. Return the saucepan to medium heat, and whisk for about 30 seconds until all of the chocolate is melted and the syrup

CONTINUED

Dirty Mocha, *continued*

is smooth. Remove from heat, cover, and set aside to cool. The syrup can be made days in advance and stored in the refrigerator.

To assemble the mocha, pour espresso into a preheated mug. Steam the milk and the dirty syrup together, reserving a little of the syrup as a garnish. Pour the steamed milk on top of the espresso. Garnish with fresh whipped cream and a drizzle of the syrup.

MAKES 1 SERVING

Those who love, and are unfortunate enough to suffer from the most universal of all gallant illnesses, will find in chocolate the most enlightening consolation.

JEAN-ANTHELEME BRILLAT-SAVARIN

Ah! How sweet coffee tastes! Lovelier than a thousand kisses, sweeter far than muscatel wine!

J.S. BACH, *COFFEE CANTATA*

Minted Mocha

Fran Bigelow, Fran's Chocolates, Seattle, Washington

The peppermint leaf has been handed down from the ancient Greeks and Romans, who used it to soothe the digestion after feast days. Today in the Yakima Valley of Washington State, the right combination of weather and soil augments the essential oil content of the fresh native leaves, boosting the taste and aroma in this rich, dark, evocative mocha, perfect for quieting the stomach after a rich meal. With the world seemingly on endless edge these days, Fran Bigelow's bracing, refreshing drink spreads a mantle of aromatic warmth that lifts spirits and reduces stress.

1 cup milk

$1/4$ ounce fresh mint leaves

2 ounces dark chocolate, (65% cacao), finely chopped

2 ounces espresso

Whipped cream, for garnish

Shaved chocolate, for garnish

In a small saucepan, bring the milk to a boil. Remove from the heat, pour into a bowl and add the fresh mint leaves. Cover tightly with plastic wrap. Steep for 10 to 12 minutes. Strain the mixture and return to the saucepan. Set over low heat, and bring to a simmer. Pour the milk over the chocolate, and stir until smooth. Divide the chocolate into 2 mugs. Pour the espresso over the chocolate. Stir to combine. Garnish with whipped cream and shaved chocolate.

MAKES 2 SERVINGS

Piedmontese

Nicole Kaplan, Eleven Madison Park, New York, New York

Each year the Union Square Hospitality Group conducts a "Barista Olympics," with waitstaff entrants from each of the company's nine restaurants. Judged on taste, visual quality, presentation, and technique in the service of signature coffees, the competitors vie for prizes that include a trip for two to Italy. Eleven Madison Park claimed bragging rights with a performance that included pastry chef Nicole Kaplan's eloquently composed drink recipe and server Jaime Marin's enthralling presentation. This latte takes its theme from the Gianduja, the legendary hazelnut-flavored chocolate from Italy's Piedmont region.

GANACHE

1 ounce Valrhona Araguani chocolate (72% cacao), coarsely chopped

4 ounces Gianduja chocolate, coarsely chopped

10 ounces milk

2 ounces espresso

HAZELNUT FOAM

7 ounces milk chocolate, chopped

7 ounces Valrhona Araguani chocolate (72% cacao), chopped

5 ounces hazelnut paste

2 1/2 cups milk

3 tablespoons corn syrup

VANILLA SAUCE

2 1/2 cups milk

1 vanilla bean, split and scraped

7 ounces half-and-half

3 1/2 ounces sugar

Pinch of salt

1 tablespoon lecithin granules

MOCHA PIEDMONTESE

15 ounces the ganache

6 ounces espresso

3 cups hazelnut foam

4 cups vanilla sauce

Cocoa powder, for garnish

Chocolate shavings, for garnish

To make the ganache, combine the two chocolates in a stainless steel bowl. In a medium saucepan, over medium-high heat, bring the milk to a boil. Pour the milk over the chocolates. Add the espresso and combine until smooth. Cover and allow to chill in the refrigerator.

To make the hazelnut foam, combine the chocolates and hazelnut paste in a medium bowl. In a medium saucepan, bring the milk and the corn syrup to a boil over medium-high heat. Pour the hot milk over the chocolates and hazelnut paste. Stir to combine. Reserve in refrigerator until ready to use.

To make the vanilla sauce, bring the milk and vanilla bean to a boil in a medium saucepan. Strain, then pour over the remaining ingredients. Stir to combine, then cover and chill until ready to use.

When you are ready to serve, combine the ganache with the hot espresso in a cocktail shaker and shake again. Add 5 ice cubes, and shake. Strain and divide among 6 glasses. Spoon the hazelnut foam over the chocolate and espresso mixture. Spoon the vanilla sauce over the hazelnut foam. Garnish with the cocoa powder and chocolate shavings.

MAKES 6 SERVINGS

Devil's Advocate

Michele Granitz, Max Crema's Espresso & Coffee Bar,
Fleetwood, Pennsylvania

Chipotles are ripe, red jalapeño peppers that have been slowly wood-smoked, and they provide a tantalizing tingle on the tongue at the finish of this creative pairing of chocolate and espresso. Created by fearless barista, Michele Granitz, the "hellfire" is tempered by the Mexican chocolate's sugar and cinnamon, while candied ginger in the whipped cream contributes a tangy sweet touch of exoticism. The lightly whipped cream prevents the volatile aromas from escaping.

CHIPOTLE CHOCOLATE SAUCE

3 ounces half-and-half

1/2 tablespoon unsalted butter

1/4 teaspoon ground chipotle pepper

1/4 pound Mexican chocolate, finely chopped, reserving a small piece to grate for garnish

1/4 teaspoon pure vanilla extract

2 teaspoons chipotle chocolate sauce

Lightly whipped heavy cream, for garnish

2 ounces espresso

Candied ginger, grated for garnish

1 lemongrass stalk, trimmed and cleaned, for garnish

To make the chipotle chocolate sauce, in the top of a double boiler over medium heat, combine the half-and-half, butter, and chipotle. Heat the mixture until a thin, papery skin appears on the top. Do not allow the mixture to boil. Add the chocolate and vanilla and stir until the chocolate melts and the mixture is smooth. Remove from the heat and let cool. This will make approximately 3/4 cup of the chocolate sauce. The remainder can be reserved for several days in the refrigerator. Be sure to bring to room temperature before using.

CONTINUED

Devil's Advocate, *continued*

Place 2 teaspoons of chocolate sauce in the bottom of cordial glass. Lightly whip the heavy cream until it forms soft peaks. Pour 2 shots of espresso into the cordial glass directly over the chocolate sauce. Stir to combine. Spoon the whipped cream on top. Garnish with grated candied ginger, grated Mexican chocolate, and the lemongrass stalk.

MAKES 1 SERVING

The damnable agent of necromancers and sorcerers. It is well to abstain from chocolate in order to avoid the familiarity and company of a nation (Spain) so suspected of sorcery.

FRENCH CLERIC, 1620

Coffee leads men to trifle away their time, scald their chops, and spend their money, all for a little base, black, thick, nasty, bitter, stinking nauseous puddle water.

THE WOMEN'S PETITION
AGAINST COFFEE, 1674

Pura Verita

Christopher Deferio, Carriage House, Ithaca, New York

The name means "simple truth" in Italian and pays homage to the land where espresso originated. "Certain things that God has created seem to have been designed, even destined, to find each other," says Christopher Deferio, an ambitious member of the contemporary barista movement. With each sip, three flavors are tasted in a harmonic succession: first the espresso, next the chocolate and cream, and finally, the star anise and mild spice at the finish.

4 star anise, smoked
1 tablespoon Earl Grey tea, loose leaf
1 tablespoon cherry wood chips
3 ounces half-and-half
3 ounces Scharffen Berger Chocolate (70% cacao), finely chopped
1 ounce espresso

To smoke the anise, line a baking pan with aluminum foil. Sprinkle the tea leaves and the wood chips on the foil. Sprinkle 2 teaspoons of water over the smoking mix. Make 4 golf ball-sized balls of foil. Place 1 ball in each corner of the baking pan. Set a fine mesh rack on the foil balls. Place the star anise on the rack. Set the baking dish on a burner over medium-high heat. When the mixture begins to produce smoke, tightly cover the dish with foil. Turn off the heat, and allow the covered mixture to smoke for 5 minutes. Remove and store in an airtight container. Carefully discard the ashes.

In a small saucepan, bring the half-and-half and 1 star anise to a slow simmer. Remove the pan from the heat, and allow to steep for 8 to10 minutes. Strain the half-and-half to remove the star anise. Return the half-and-half to the heat, and bring to a simmer.

CONTINUED

Pour the hot liquid over the chocolate, and whisk continuously until the mixture is smooth with a high gloss, about 5 minutes. Add the espresso and stir to combine.

MAKES 1 SERVING

The confection made of Cacao. . . is of wonderful efficacy for the procreation of children, for it not only vehemently incites to Venus, but causes conception in women. . . and besides that it preserves health, for it makes such as take it often to become fat and corpulent, fair and amiable.

WILLIAM COLES, *ADAM AND EVE*, 1657

Mocha Cadienne

Teri Bryant, The Black Drop, Bellingham, Washington

Italians refer to the "four m's" of espresso: *macinazione* (the grind), *miscela* (the bean), *macchina* (the machine), and *mano* (the skilled hand). Black Drop barista Teri Bryant is the skilled hand behind a drink inspired by the *Cadienne* or Cajun practice of sweetening coffee with dark or black-strap molasses. Twice-boiled sugarcane produces the rich, deep-flavored dark molasses; a third boiling produces the blackstrap, liberating robust bittersweet flavors that explode in the mouth. Teri Bryant suggests her macchiato be served as a dessert drink, perhaps accompanied by a shortbread-style cookie.

1 teaspoon molasses, dark or blackstrap

1 teaspoon Guittard Dark Chocolate Syrup

2 ounces espresso

Cocoa powder, unsweetened

Whole milk

Combine the molasses and chocolate syrup in a demitasse cup. Add 2 shots of espresso, straight from the machine into the cup. Combine gently to preserve as much crema as possible. Sprinkle cocoa powder over the coffee mixture. In a steaming pitcher, steam the milk to 140°F to a latte consistency. By the time the milk is finished, the chocolate shavings should be absorbed into the crema of the espresso. Pour the milk quickly into the cup to avoid separation. Gradually add the foam against the opposite side of the cup (this gets easier with practice), and finish by pulling the stream of milk through the foam to create a heart. Serve on a saucer with a demitasse spoon.

MAKES 1 SERVING

Baroque

Danielle Coleman, Cocoa Connoisseur, Spring, Texas

Seventeenth-century Italian, Francesco Redi, was a scientist, poet, physician, and *cioccolatieri* to the Grand Duke of Tuscany who infused flavored drinks for the Tuscan court with sweetly scented jasmine flowers. Danielle Coleman gently perfumes a familiar fusion of chocolate and coffee *con panna* with a dollop of fragrant, jasmine-sweetened whipped cream. It is a bittersweet, rich, and floral restorative.

1/2 cup heavy cream

4 tablespoons Monin Jasmine Syrup

2 ounces espresso

2 teaspoons unsweetened cocoa powder

1 teaspoon sugar

In a mixing bowl, whip the heavy cream until slightly thickened. Add the jasmine syrup and continue whipping until cream begins to hold its shape.

Pour the espresso over the cocoa powder in the bottom of a brandy snifter. Stir until smooth and thoroughly dissolved. Stir in the sugar. Spoon the jasmine syrup-infused whipped cream on top. Serve immediately.

MAKES 1 SERVING

Mocha Azteca

Brent Fortune, Crema Coffee & Bakery, Portland, Oregon

Legend has it that Spanish conquistador Hernando Cortes was introduced to vanilla as an ingredient in drinking chocolate served at the table of Aztec king Montezuma. Vanilla supplies provocative aromatics to this barista's interpretation of *café au lait,* combining Mexican chocolate with dark-roasted, full-flavored espresso. Traditional Mexican chocolate, with almonds, cinnamon, and sugar, brings theatrical energy to the collaboration, but Brent Fortune warns that coffee flavor is easily lost in combination with other ingredients. "Take care not to mask the espresso," he advises, "and adjust the measurements according to taste."

MOCHA AZTECA

1 ounce Ibarra chocolate, coarsely chopped

1/2 ounce vanilla bean syrup

2 ounces espresso

6 ounces steamed whole milk

Chocolate curls, for garnish

Cocoa powder, for garnish

VANILLA BEAN SYRUP

8 ounces water

1 cup plus 2 tablespoons sugar

1 Tahitian vanilla bean, split and scraped

To make the vanilla bean syrup, in a medium saucepan, combine the water and sugar and stir to ensure all the sugar is moistened. Over medium-high heat, bring the mixture to a boil, stirring occasionally to dissolve the sugar. After the sugar and water come to a boil, add the vanilla bean. Remove the pan from the heat, cover, and let steep for 20 minutes. Strain to remove the vanilla pod.

Add the chocolate pieces to a pre-heated mug and then add the vanilla bean syrup. Pour the espresso over the chocolate-vanilla bean syrup mixture and stir to combine. Gently steam the milk and pour over the espresso. Stir gently. Garnish with chocolate curls or a dusting of cocoa.

MAKES 1 SERVING

Mocha Flip

Heather Perry, Coffee Klatch, San Dimas, California

She was the 2003 American Barista Champion—coffee culture's version of *Iron Chef*—in a competition that judges technical skills, speed, and taste. Heather Perry calls her profession "an art, a craft, and a passion." Her best drinks mingle the comfort of the familiar with a dash of experimentation or a dollop of whimsy. She considers this drink her "ultimate sipper," an eye-opening potion inspired by the formula of an old-school cocktail.

ORANGE WHIPPED CREAM

1/2 cup heavy cream

1/8 teaspoon pure orange extract

1 tablespoon powdered sugar

MOCHA FLIP

4 egg yolks

3 tablespoons confectioners' sugar

2 tablespoons shaved bittersweet (60%) chocolate

4 ounces espresso

To make the whipped cream, combine the heavy cream, orange extract, and powdered sugar and whip until it forms soft (not stiff) peaks.

Beat the egg yolks until they are thin and runny (like water). Combine with the confectioners' sugar in a double boiler over medium heat. Add the chocolate and whisk until mixture becomes smooth and creamy. Pull 4 shots of espresso and stir into the egg mixture. Divide among 4 small glasses. Top each with a small amount of whipped cream and serve immediately.

MAKES 4 SERVINGS

Zen Mocha

Phuong Tran, Lava Java Café, Ridgefield, Washington

In addition to running a coffee bar in southwest Washington, Phuong Tran is a national champion and superstar on the barista competition circuit. Borrowing from her Vietnamese background, she has an exotic way with ingredients and a sure grasp of Southeast Asian techniques. She invigorates this mocha-inspired drink with the alluring flavor of lemongrass for an unexpected taste. Cold does not transfer flavor as well as heat, so the iced drink depends on a strong espresso brew, high-quality chocolate, and fresh lemongrass.

LEMONGRASS-CHOCOLATE PURÉE

4 ounces semi-sweet chocolate, finely chopped

1/2 cup heavy cream

1 fresh lemongrass stalk, coarsely chopped

LEMONGRASS SYRUP

2 fresh lemongrass stalks, finely chopped

6 ounces water

1 teaspoon honey

ZEN MOCHA

1/2 cup lemongrass-chocolate purée

3/4 cup lemongrass syrup

1 lemon, sliced very thin

6 ounces espresso

6 fresh lemongrass stalks, clean and trimmed, for garnish

To make the lemongrass-chocolate purée, place the chocolate in a small bowl. In a small saucepan over medium heat, bring the cream and lemongrass to a boil. Strain the mixture directly onto the chocolate. Discard the lemongrass. Gently whisk the chocolate and cream until smooth. Set aside to cool.

To make the lemongrass syrup, in a small saucepan, combine the lemongrass, water, and honey and bring to a boil. Reduce the heat and bring the mixture to a simmer. Simmer for 4 minutes. Strain and set aside to cool.

Combine lemongrass purée, lemongrass syrup, lemon slices, and espresso in a chilled cocktail shaker. Fill the shaker with ice cubes and shake well. Fill 6 glasses with ice cubes. Strain the mixture into the chilled glasses over the ice cubes. Garnish with fresh lemongrass stalks as stir sticks.

MAKES 6 SERVINGS

Last comes the beverage of the Orient shore, Mocha, far off, the fragrant berries bore. Taste the dark fluid with a dainty lip. Digestion waits on pleasure as you sip.

POPE LEO XII

Mocha Frappé

Elizabeth Katz, B.R. Guest Restaurants, New York, New York

Baking for her family's gourmet food shop in New Rochelle, New York, Elizabeth Katz was introduced to high-end desserts early in life. Her extensive knowledge of ingredients combined with a flair for the creative has allowed her to ascend to a career as executive pastry chef for Stephen Hanson's fourteen New York City restaurants. This refreshing frappé explores the relationship of chocolate and coffee by layering chocolate gelato, arbol chile-spiced cream, citrus soda, and espresso granita.

CHOCOLATE GELATO

3 cups milk

1 cup heavy cream

1/2 cup sugar

4 egg yolks

2 tablespoons cocoa powder

1 cup bittersweet chocolate, finely chopped

SPICED CREAM

1 small arbol chile, dried

1 cup heavy cream

2 tablespoons confectioners' sugar

ESPRESSO GRANITA

3 cups water

1/2 cup instant espresso powder

3/4 cup granulated sugar

MOCHA FRAPPÉ

3 cups chocolate gelato

1 cup spiced cream

5 cups citrus soda water

3 cups espresso granita

Zest of 1 orange

To make the chocolate gelato, in a medium saucepan, combine the milk, cream, and 1/4 cup of sugar. Bring the mixture to a boil. While the milk is heating, in a mixing bowl, whisk the egg yolks with the remaining 1/4 cup of sugar. Remove the milk from the heat. Slowly whisk $1/2$ cup of the hot milk-cream mixture into the egg yolks. Whisk together to combine completely. Pour all of the warmed egg mixture into the hot cream mixture, whisk to combine. Return the milk and egg mixture to the heat. Whisk in the cocoa powder and chopped bittersweet chocolate. Cook over low heat, stirring continuously until the mixture is thickened, the chocolate is melted, and the mixture is smooth. Remove from the heat and strain. Set aside and allow to cool completely. Pour the cooled mixture into an ice cream machine and follow the manufacturer's instructions. Once frozen, remove the gelato mixture from the machine and place it in a chilled container and place it in the freezer

To make the spiced cream, split the arbol chile open and remove the seeds. Crush the chile into a powder using a mortar and pestle or a rolling pin. Whip the cream until it forms soft peaks. Fold in the confectioners' sugar and the chile powder. Reserve in refrigerator until ready to serve.

To make the espresso granita, in a medium saucepan, bring the water to a boil. Add the instant espresso and the granulated sugar and stir to dissolve. Pour the mixture into a shallow baking pan and place in the freezer to freezer. Remove from the freezer every 30 minutes and scrape with a fork. Continue this process until all the liquid has frozen and formed little crystals of espresso ice.

To assemble the mocha frappé, place $1/2$ cup of the chocolate gelato into the bottom of a large soda or ice cream glass. Add the spiced cream. Pour in citrus soda, filling the glass almost to the top. Finally, add the espresso granita and sprinkle the top with the orange zest. Repeat for each serving. Serve with a spoon and straw.

MAKES 6 SERVINGS

A Cup a Day . . .

Chocolate contains phenylethylamine, the same chemical released by the body during moments of romantic love and physical arousal. When we drink chocolate, the phenylethylamine enters the system, causing a rise in blood pressure, increased heart rate, and inducing feelings of overall well being, bordering on euphoria. This once-mysterious phenomenon explains chocolate's mood-elevating and libido-enhancing effects.

On the other hand, the caffeine in coffee enhances alertness and motivation, facilitates thought formation and concentration, and decreases mental fatigue. One or two cups of coffee can make you feel more alert and able to concentrate.

In combination, coffee and chocolate have a complimentary effect. One wakes you up, and the other puts you in a good mood. Additionally, a number of bona fide health benefits attributed to chocolate and coffee have been confirmed by medical research. At Cornell University, studies have shown that chocolate contains high levels of cell-protecting antioxidants—vitamins C and E and beta carotene, in particular—widely believed to boost the immune system, fight cancer, and restrict the formation of the type of cholesterol that damages the heart.

Cocktails

Pharisee

Wilhelm and Melanie Wanders, Chocolaterie Wanders, Washington, D.C.

One version or another of this European drink has been served at a Wanders family *konditorei* (pastry shop) for generations. Next in a long line of German *konditormeisters,* Wilhelm and Melanie Wanders continue the family tradition of artisan confections in Washington, D.C. His version balances espresso with the deep chocolate flavor of Valrhona Caraque. He recommends chilling the milk, espresso, and chocolate mixture before reheating to produce a creamier, richer tasting drink, and he favors Cockspur rum for its extremely smooth finish. (For a sweeter version, replace half of the bittersweet chocolate with your favorite milk chocolate.)

3/4 cup whole milk

3/4 cup espresso or strong coffee

1 cup Valrhona Caraque or other bittersweet chocolate, chopped

1/2 cup Rum

1/4 cup heavy cream, whipped to soft peaks

Dash of ground cinnamon

2 cinnamon sticks, for garnish

In a small saucepan, combine the milk and espresso. Bring the mixture to a boil over medium-high heat. Remove the saucepan from the heat; add the chocolate, whisking to combine. Allow the chocolate mixture to cool for 15 minutes at room temperature. Cover and refrigerate for at least 2 hours. When ready to serve, gently heat the mixture, uncovered, over medium-low heat, stirring continuously, until warmed through. Add the rum, stirring to combine. Evenly divide the mixture between 2 mugs. Top each mug with a dollop of whipped cream. Dust with ground cinnamon and serve with a cinnamon stick in each mug for garnish.

Café Exagerado

Paul Tanguay, Sushi Samba, New York, Miami, Chicago, Tel-Aviv

The Sushi Samba brainchild is based on a highly evolved fusion of Asian and South American cultures and cuisines, fostered by the thousands of Japanese who immigrated to Peru and Brazil, mostly at the beginning of the twentieth century. Multicultural influences come naturally to Paul Tanguay, the French-Canadian beverage director of the restaurants, who uses a small-batch, wood-aged Brazilian *cachaça* (kah-SHAH-sah) to "exaggerate" the mix of espresso and chocolate liqueur. Richly nuanced GRM cachaça, distilled from pure sugarcane juice, adds cinnamon and vanilla flavors to the dessert cocktail.

1 ounce cachaça (GRM preferred)

1 ounce Godiva White Chocolate Liqueur

1 ounce espresso, cooled to room temperature

1 ounce simple syrup (see Caffé Shakerato con Cioccolato, page 40, for recipe)

1 egg white

Angustura bitters

Into a cocktail shaker prepared with cracked ice, add the cachaça, chocolate liqueur, espresso, simple syrup, and egg white. Shake vigorously until the contents are thoroughly combined and chilled. Strain into a chilled cocktail glass and over the top squirt 2 dashes of bitters.

MAKES 1 SERVING

Resurrección

Tony Abou-Ganim, The Modern Mixologist, Las Vegas, Nevada

As a master bartender, Tony Abou-Ganim has developed cocktail programs for San Francisco's Balboa Café and the Bellagio in Las Vegas. For a cocktail to complement spicy cuisine, he begins with the base of Peruvian Pisco. "Made from Muscat-style grapes, this unaged brandy screams of fresh ripe grapes, melon, and tropical fruits," he explains. "It becomes a perfect compliment to the chocolate-coffee liaison, especially with a slight rich, bitter note from the Fernet Branca." Traditionally known as a wonderful digestive, the Fernet Branca balances the cocoa and espresso and stands up well to hot and spicy foods.

CHOCOLATE-ESPRESSO SAUCE

1 cup water
1/4 cup unsweetened cocoa
1/4 cup instant espresso powder
1/2 cup granulated sugar
Pinch of salt

RESURRECCIÓN

1 1/2 ounce Barsol Pisco Italia
1/4 ounce Fernet Branca
1 1/2 ounce chocolate-espresso sauce
1/2 ounce heavy cream
Sprig of rosemary, for garnish

To make the chocolate-espresso sauce, in a small saucepan, bring the water to a boil and dissolve the cocoa, espresso powder, sugar, and salt completely. Allow to cool and refrigerate until needed, up to one week.

To assemble the drink, into a cocktail shaker prepared with cracked ice, pour the Pisco, Fernet Branca, chocolate-espresso sauce, and cream. Shake vigorously until the contents are thoroughly combined and chilled. Strain into chilled cocktail glass and over the top, float a sprig of rosemary.

MAKES 1 SERVING

Caribbean Rum Truffle

Whitney Pallend, Cuchi Cuchi, Cambridge, Massachusetts

From behind the grand mahogany bar of this civilized preserve, bartender Whitney Pallend constructs an imaginative cocktail that adds a rich complexity of flavors to espresso and chocolate liqueurs with the reinforcement of Rhum Barbancourt from Haiti. Pressed from the juice of sugarcane, distilled in copper alembic stills, then aged for fifteen years in French limousine oak casks, the rum adds notes of caramel and honey and a brandy-like bouquet. This drink mellows as the ingredients mingle in the glass and matures with each sip.

2 ounces Rhum Barbancourt

1¼ ounces Godiva Dark Chocolate Liqueur

¾ ounce White Crème de Cacao

1½ ounces espresso, cooled to room temperature

Ground nutmeg

Into a cocktail shaker prepared with cracked ice, pour the rum, chocolate liqueur, crème de cacao, and espresso. Shake vigorously until the contents are thoroughly combined and chilled. Strain into a pre-chilled martini glass rimmed with nutmeg.

MAKES 1 SERVING

The Mocha

Ian Farquhar, Dessert Noir Café & Bar, Beaverton, Oregon

Pastry chef Ian Farquhar shakes things up at his sweets-centric restaurant with a martini-inspired dessert—a composition of espresso spiked with cocoa-infused vodka, sweetened with both dark and white chocolate liqueurs. The presentation is artfully enhanced with a "crusta," so called because the rim of the glass is moistened with chocolate syrup, then dipped into cocoa powder, forming a pleasing crust around the rim. It's fairly sweet, so be sure to step up the espresso if a drier drink is desired.

CHOCOLATE SYRUP

1 cup Valrhona Cocoa Powder

1 1/2 cups sugar

Dash of salt

1 1/2 cups water

1 teaspoon vanilla extract

MOCHA

2 shots of Three Olives Chocolate Vodka

1 shot of Godiva Dark Chocolate Liqueur

1 shot of Godiva White Chocolate Liqueur

1 shot of fresh-brewed espresso

Chocolate syrup, for rimming the cocktail glass

Cocoa powder, for garnish

To make the chocolate syrup, in a saucepan, combine the cocoa, sugar, salt, and water. Boil 2 to 5 minutes, stirring rapidly, until sauce begins to thicken. Remove from the heat and set aside to cool. When cool, stir in the vanilla.

MAKES 2 CUPS OF SYRUP

CONTINUED

The Mocha, *continued*

Pour a small amount of the chocolate syrup into a saucer. Dip the rim of a chilled martini glass into the chocolate sauce and gently turn the glass to coat the rim. Re-chill the chocolate-rimmed glass until ready to serve.

Fill a cocktail shaker with ice and pour the vodka, liqueurs, and espresso into the shaker. Shake vigorously for a few seconds until the ingredients are combined. Strain into the re-chilled, chocolate-rimmed martini glass and garnish with cocoa powder. Serve immediately.

MAKES 1 SERVING

The voodoo priest and all his powders were as nothing compared to espresso, cappuccino, and mocha, which are stronger than all the religions of the world combined, and perhaps stronger than the human soul itself.

MARK HELPRIN, *MEMOIR FROM ANTPROOF CASE*

Mocca con Mosca

Rose Parrotta, Happy Rooster, Philadelphia, Pennsylvania

Adding liqueur to a chocolate-coffee combination provides intoxicating warmth to an after-dinner drink. *Caffé corretto,* or "corrected coffee," as the Italians say, is a combination that's simple yet beguiling, and impossible to tire of. Sambuca, the traditional Italian digestive, flavored with anise, elderberries, and lemon, amplifies this mocha blend, especially when garnished with three coffee beans *con mosca* (literally, "with flies"), representing health, wealth, and happiness At this legendary Philadelphia bistro, you're encouraged to chew on the bitter beans between sips to balance the sweetness of the liqueur.

1 ounce bittersweet chocolate, finely shaved

2 tablespoons boiling water

2 ounces espresso

1 1/2 ounces Opal Nera, or other black sambuca

Heavy cream

3 coffee beans

In a small bowl, combine the chocolate shavings with boiling water and stir until smooth. Pour into the bottom of a snifter, then add the espresso and the sambuca, and stir. Pour a thin layer of heavy cream (shaken to the consistency of French yogurt) over the top. Add coffee beans and serve immediately.

MAKES 1 SERVING

Chocolate Espresso Martini

Kathy Casey, Kathy Casey Food Studios, Seattle, Washington

To many of us, the martini is gin and dry vermouth. But according to Seattle's cocktail and culinary diva and "Dishing" columnist for *The Seattle Times,* when it comes to the vodka martini, there is a wide assortment of impetuous variations that carry its name. So when asked to explore chocolate and coffee in the framework of a modern martini, Kathy Casey connected the ingredients with a delicate cream liqueur made from the fruit pulp of the African marula tree. Check your local liquor store for availability (or substitute Bailey's Irish Cream Liqueur).

COCKTAIL PRE-MIX

1/2 cup Starbucks Coffee Liqueur

1/2 cup Amarula Cream

3 tablespoons high-quality chocolate sauce, such as Fran's or Scharffen Berger

1/2 cup vanilla vodka

CHOCOLATE CREAM

1/3 cup whipping cream

2 tablespoons chocolate sauce

Chocolate-covered espresso beans

To make the pre-mix, in a small container, combine the coffee liqueur, Amarula, chocolate sauce, and vodka. Transfer to a pretty bottle with a pour spout. The pre-mix can be made up to 1 week in advance if kept refrigerated.

To make the whipped cream, in a small bowl, combine the whipping cream and chocolate sauce and whip until very, very soft peaks are formed.

To make the cocktail, fill a cocktail shaker with ice and then measure and add 2 ounces (1/4 cup) of the pre-mix. Shake vigorously for 10 seconds, then strain into a small martini glass. Top each cocktail with a dollop of the whipped cream and garnish with chocolate-covered coffee beans.

MAKES 6 SERVINGS

Cara Sposa

Ann Amernick, Palena, Washington, D.C.

Before opening Palena, Ann Amernick cooked at the White House for presidents Carter and Reagan, then at Jean-Louis at the Watergate. The acclaimed pastry legend puts her sweet stamp on an Italian after-dinner drink that creates a marriage of flavorful equals (its name translates to "beloved spouse"). She adds Grand Marnier Cordon Rouge, the blend of cognac and distilled essence of orange, to seal the deal. The selection of Valrhona Caraibe cleverly matches the chocolate's intense taste, the sustained fullness of the coffee, and hints of dried fruits from the liqueur.

MOCHA

2 ounces Grand Marnier or fine cognac

1 teaspoon sugar

8 ounces of hot coffee

8 ounces hot chocolate

1/2 cup heavy cream

2 tablespoons grated chocolate

HOT CHOCOLATE

3/4 cup whole milk

1/4 cup heavy cream

2 tablespoons sugar

4 ounces bittersweet chocolate (66% Valrhona Caraibe)

1/2 teaspoon vanilla extract

To make the hot chocolate, in a small, heavy saucepan combine all of the ingredients. Set over high heat, stirring constantly, until the chocolate is melted and the ingredients are incorporated.

In a saucepan, stir the liqueur, sugar, hot coffee, and hot chocolate until thoroughly combined. Heat gently (do not boil it). Divide the mixture between 2 cups. Top each cup with the heavy cream and dust with grated chocolate.

MAKES 2 SERVINGS

Fireside Chat

Emily Luchetti, Farallon, San Francisco, California

Cozying up in front of a roaring fireplace on a cold winter's night is one of life's simple pleasures. To gain the most from this experience, Emily Luchetti proposes a heartwarming elixir of chocolate and coffee elevated with the rich, fragrant flavors of Italian hazelnut liqueur. Frangelico is produced in the Piedmont region of Northern Italy, its origins dating back more than three hundred years when it was first made from toasted hazelnuts, cocoa, vanilla berries, and rhubarb root.

$^2/_3$ cup cream

$^3/_4$ cup milk

5 ounces white chocolate, chopped

3 ounces milk chocolate, chopped

2 tablespoons cocoa powder

$2^1/_4$ cups hot espresso or rich coffee

9 tablespoons Frangelico

In a small saucepan, heat the cream and milk until hot. Turn off the heat and add the white and milk chocolate pieces. Let sit for several minutes, then whisk until smooth. Whisk in the cocoa. Stir in the espresso and Frangelico. Serve hot in pre-warmed mugs.

MAKES 6 SERVINGS

My Breakfast with Vermeer

Christian Balbierer, Chocolate Pink Café, Atlanta, Georgia

An artist in his own right, Chef Christian Balbierer is dedicated to elevating chocolate from a craft into an edible art form. Vermeer Dutch Chocolate Cream, named after the great Dutch Master Johannes Vermeer, is a richly-flavored chocolate liqueur that brings an Old-World harmony to a modern-day recipe. To complete the experience, the chef provides bittersweet chocolate chip donuts for dunking. (A day-old donut is best for dunking since it doesn't fall apart easily in the liquid.)

3 cups whole milk

2 cups half-and-half

2 tablespoons cane sugar

3/4 cup coffee beans, whole, medium roast

1 cup milk chocolate (38% cacao), plus more for shaving

5 ounces Vermeer liqueur

Milk chocolate shavings, for garnish

2 pinches fleur de sel, for garnish

In a medium saucepan over medium-high heat, combine 2 cups of the whole milk, the half-and-half, and the sugar, and bring just to a boil. Remove from the heat and add the coffee beans. Cover with plastic wrap and set aside to steep for 15 minutes. Return to low heat, stirring occasionally, until the mixture reaches a simmer. Remove from the heat, add the chocolate, and stir with a wooden spoon until completely melted and smooth. Add the liqueur, and stir to combine. Pour the mixture into a French press. In a small saucepan heat the remaining 1 cup of milk until hot to the touch, remove from heat and froth with a steamer or immersion blender. Press the milk chocolate mixture and divide among 6 mugs. Place a spoonful of the frothed milk on top of each. Garnish with shaved milk chocolate and a sprinkle of fleur de sel.

MAKES 6 SERVINGS

Chocolate Chip Donuts

1³/4 cups warm water

2 envelopes active dry yeast

1 Madagascar vanilla bean, split and
    scraped, seeds only

3³/4 cups pastry flour, sifted

2 tablespoons sugar

³/4 teaspoon salt

³/4 cup Santander Bittersweet Chocolate
    (65% cacao), finely chopped

24 ounces canola oil, for frying

1 tablespoon confectioners' sugar

2 tablespoons dark cocoa powder

In a large mixing bowl, whisk the warm water with the yeast and vanilla bean seeds until well combined. Let stand for 5 minutes. Using a wooden spoon, stir in the sifted flour, sugar, and salt. Stir until thoroughly combined. Scrape the dough out onto a lightly floured surface. Add the chopped chocolate and knead lightly until dough is silky in appearance. Lightly oil a medium bowl and place the dough in it. Cover with plastic wrap and set in a warm place to rise, about 1¹/2 hours or until doubled in volume. Once the dough has doubled, punch it down, then let the dough rise again for 30 minutes. In a large saucepan, using a thermometer, bring the canola oil to 325°F. Divide the dough into quarters. Cut each quarter into 10 pieces. With damp hands, shape the dough into balls. Carefully add the doughnuts to the oil, several at a time, and fry until golden brown, about 1 minute per side. Drain on paper towels. When still slightly warm, combine the confectioners' sugar and cocoa powder and sift over the doughnuts.

MAKES 18 DONUTS

Desserts

Mocha-Java Cheesecake

Melissa Murphy, Sweet Melissa Patisserie, Brooklyn, New York

Before opening her French country-style patisserie in a tiny Brooklyn storefront, Melissa Murphy made a name for herself baking desserts for many of New York's City's finest restaurants. "This cheesecake originated during the cigar bar phenomenon," she explains, "when desserts needed to complement the prevailing ambiance." Rich and decadent, this silky, delicious cheesecake is the perfect way to finish off a meal, alongside a snifter of cognac and a good cigar.

CRUST

1/2 cup flour

2 tablespoons cocoa powder

1/2 teaspoon salt

1/2 cup sugar

1/4 cup hazelnuts, chopped medium fine

3 tablespoons butter, melted

1/4 cup semisweet chocolate chips

CHEESECAKE

8 ounces bittersweet chocolate, melted

3/4 cup heavy cream

4 teaspoons cocoa powder

2 tablespoons instant espresso powder

1/4 teaspoon salt

1 pound cream cheese, room temperature

3/4 cup sugar

2 eggs

1/4 cup dark rum

Place a rack in the middle of your oven. Preheat oven to 325°F. Turn an 8-inch springform pan upside down and cover the outside bottom of the pan with aluminum foil so that it is water proofed at least 3 inches up the sides of the pan. The pan will be baking in a water bath. Line the inside bottom of the springform pan with parchment paper cut to fit exactly. Using a nonstick vegetable spray,

CONTINUED

grease the inside papered bottom and sides of the springform pan.

To make the crust, combine the flour, cocoa powder, salt, sugar, and hazelnuts in a medium bowl. Stir in the melted butter. Press this mixture into the bottom and 1 inch up the sides of the springform pan. Use a cup with a flat base to help press the crumbs evenly up the sides of the pan.

Bake the crust for 15 minutes. Remove the crust from the oven and immediately scatter the chocolate chips onto the crust. Set aside until the chocolate melts, about 4 minutes. Spread the melted chocolate evenly over the crust using a small offset spatula or a teaspoon. Set aside to cool. Reduce the oven to 300°F.

To make the cheesecake, melt the chocolate over a double boiler and keep the chocolate warm once it has melted. In a small, heavy saucepan, whisk together the heavy cream, cocoa powder, espresso powder, and salt. Stir over low heat until the mixture comes to a boil. Remove from heat and set aside to cool slightly.

In the bowl of an electric mixer fitted with the paddle attachment, combine the cream cheese and the sugar on medium speed, until smooth, scraping the bowl and paddle frequently. Add the melted chocolate and continue to mix until smooth. Scrape the bottom of the bowl, and add the cream-cocoa mixture until thoroughly combined. Scrape the bowl and paddle again.

Add the eggs, one at a time, and stir until just combined. Add the rum and stir until combined. Pour the cheesecake batter into the prepared crust. Cover with foil.

Place the cheesecake in a roasting pan. Fill the roasting pan with hot water reaching halfway up the sides of the pan. Bake for 60 minutes, then reduce the oven to 250°F and bake for an additional 45 minutes, or until almost set. Turn the oven off. *Without removing the cheese-*

cake from the oven, remove the foil from the top of the cheesecake, and let the cheesecake finish in the still oven for 1 additional hour. Do not open the oven door during this final hour.

Remove the cheesecake from the oven. Carefully remove the foil (a few teaspoons of water may have pooled in the foil cover) and set cheesecake on a rack to cool to room temperature. Refrigerate for three hours or overnight. To unmold, slide a knife along the edge of the cheesecake and release the springform. Remove from the base using 2 offset spatulas and transfer to a serving plate.

MAKES 8 TO 10 SERVINGS

Carefully prepared chocolate is as healthful a food as it is pleasant; that it is nourishing and easily digested; that it does not cause the same harmful effects to feminine beauty which are blamed on coffee, but is on the contrary a remedy for them.

JEAN-ANTHELEME BRILLAT-SAVARIN

Mocha Biscotti

Joanne Chang, Flour Bakery + Café, Boston, Massachusetts

Joanne Chang is a Harvard grad who gave up management consulting for a career in the pastry kitchen. After a stint at New York City's acclaimed Payard Patisserie, she opened a neighborhood bakery and café in Boston's South End, where she advances the Italian art of dunking with crisp, subtle, and slightly sweet mocha biscotti. First made in the Tuscan city of Prato, where dunking is a time-honored tradition, twice-baked biscotti have become an essential part of café culture. Biscotti will keep a long time if stored in an airtight tin.

3 eggs

1 cup sugar

3 tablespoons instant espresso powder

1 tablespoon vanilla

2$^1/_2$ cups all-purpose flour

1 teaspoon baking powder

$^1/_4$ teaspoon salt

3 tablespoons espresso grounds

1 cup bittersweet chocolate, chopped

Preheat oven to 350°F. In a large mixing bowl, whip together the eggs and sugar until thick and light, at least 10 minutes. Add the espresso powder and vanilla and whip another few minutes. In a separate bowl, combine the flour, baking powder, salt, and espresso grounds. Fold the egg mixture and flour mixture together, then fold in the chopped chocolate. Shape the dough into a single strip about 3 inches wide and place onto a cookie sheet lined with parchment or waxed paper. Bake until golden brown and baked through, about 30 to 40 minutes. Let cool. When cool enough to handle, slice thinly and spread out on a cookie sheet. Re-bake sliced biscotti at 200°F for 4 to 5 hours until baked through. Remove the baking sheet from the oven and transfer to a cooling rack.

MAKES 18 TO 20 BISCOTTI

Chocolate and the King are my only passions.

PRINCESS MARIA THERESA
OF AUSTRIA

Make my coffee like I like my men: hot, black, and strong.

WILLONA WOOD, *GOOD TIMES*

Kaffee Schokolade Coffeecake

Dufflet Rosenberg, Dufflet Pastries, Toronto

The close link between coffee and cake can be traced to the Viennese *kaffee-konditorei*—half coffeeshop, half pastry shop— where you can relax, read the newspaper, and enjoy some coffee. A proper accompaniment might resemble a moist cake with just enough coffee aromatics and chocolate chunks to lift the spirits. It makes a perfect breakfast splurge, light dessert, or nighttime treat. Although it is best served the same day at room temperature, it can be kept for up to three days at room temperature or refrigerated if well wrapped.

CAKE BATTER

3 cups flour

1 1/2 teaspoons baking powder

1 1/2 teaspoons baking soda

3/4 teaspoon salt

3/4 cup butter, unsalted

1 1/2 cups brown sugar, packed

3 large eggs

4 teaspoons instant espresso

2 teaspoons vanilla extract

1 1/2 cups full-fat sour cream

FILLING

3/4 cup brown sugar, packed

1/2 cup pecans, toasted and chopped

1 tablespoon instant espresso

1/2 cup chocolate chunks or large chocolate chips

CHOCOLATE GLAZE

3 to 6 tablespoons heavy cream, or until a drizzling consistency

2 ounces semi-sweet chocolate

Preheat oven to 325°F. Grease and flour a large, 10-cup tube pan.

To make the filling, combine the sugar, pecans, espresso, and chocolate in a bowl and set aside.

CONTINUED

To make the cake batter, in a large bowl, combine the flour, baking powder, baking soda, and salt, and set aside. In a separate bowl, on medium speed, cream the butter and sugar until light and fluffy. Beat in the eggs, one at a time, beating well after each addition and scraping down the sides of bowl as needed. In a separate bowl, dissolve the espresso into the vanilla extract, then add to the egg mixture. On low speed, add the dry (flour) mixture alternately with the sour cream in 3 additions, ending with the dry.

To assemble the cake, scrape half the batter into the prepared pan and smooth with a spatula. Sprinkle half of the filling over the batter. Cover with the remaining batter and smooth. Top with the remaining filling. Bake in center of the oven until tester comes out clean, approximately 1 hour. Let cool in the pan until still warm. Remove from the pan to continue cooling.

To make the glaze, in a small saucepan, bring the cream to a simmer and then pour over the chopped chocolate. Stir until blended. Drizzle cake with slightly warm chocolate glaze.

MAKES 10 TO 12 SERVINGS

Affogato, Southeast Asian–Style

Tina Luu, The Art Institute of California, San Diego, California

Preparing an original dessert is like painting a fine portrait. The artist, in this case, is pastry chef Tina Luu. Tina has combined the best of two worlds with energy and style—Asian innovation meets Italian tradition—in this conjuring of ice cream and coffee. Her iconoclastic dessert drowns a Thai basil-accented chocolate ice cream in two shots of inky black espresso. "You could do straight basil or you could do half with fresh mint," suggests Ms. Luu. "Either way is nice." The dish is finished with cocoa syrup and whipped cream, accompanied by Vietnamese shortbread cookies in place of traditional biscotti.

ICE CREAM

3 cups whole milk

1 ounce fresh Thai basil leaves, crushed

Pinch of salt

$1^1/2$ ounces Valrhona Cocoa Powder

11 ounces sugar

8 egg yolks

1 cup heavy cream

COCOA SYRUP

$3^3/4$ ounces Valrhona Cocoa Powder

7 ounces sugar

Pinch of salt

1 cup water, boiling

$1/2$ teaspoon vanilla extract

CONTINUED

VIETNAMESE SHORTBREAD AU CAFÉ

1 pound butter

1 tablespoon instant espresso powder

7 ounces sugar

1/4 teaspoon kosher salt

1/4 vanilla bean, scraped

1 pound 4 ounces all-purpose flour

Confectioners' sugar for dusting

12 ounces espresso

To make the ice cream, combine the milk, basil, and salt in a saucepan and bring to a boil. Remove from the heat and set aside to infuse for 15 minutes. In a mixing bowl, combine the cocoa powder and sugar. Strain the milk mixture and return to the saucepan. Add the cocoa powder and sugar to the milk and bring to a boil, stirring constantly. In a separate bowl, whisk the egg yolks to a pale ribbon. Gradually add the hot liquid into the yolks. Return the mixture to the saucepan and stir over medium-high heat for 30 seconds. Turn the heat off and immediately add the cream. Strain through a fine cheesecloth. Place the saucepan in an ice bath to cool. When thoroughly cooled, transfer to an ice cream maker and freeze according to the manufacturers instructions.

MAKES 1 1/2 QUARTS

To make the cocoa syrup, combine the cocoa powder, sugar, and salt in a saucepan. Add enough boiling water to make a thick, smooth paste. Add the remaining water and whisk until smooth. Bring the mixture to a simmer and stir 1 minute. Remove from the heat and add the vanilla. Strain through a cheesecloth.

MAKES 1 CUP

To make the shortbread, cream the butter, espresso powder, sugar, and salt just until smooth. Do not beat too much air into it. Add the vanilla bean and combine. Add half of the flour and combine with the butter. Add the remaining flour and mix only until it comes together. Wrap in plastic wrap and chill the dough for at least 2 hours. On a floured surface, roll the dough out to $1/6$ to $1/4$ inch and cut into desired cookie shapes. Chill the cut dough while the oven preheats. Bake at 325°F until lightly golden brown and firm to the touch. Set aside to cool. When cooled, dust lightly with confectioners' sugar.

MAKES 24 COOKIES

Serve in 4 one-pint or half-pint glasses by drizzling the cocoa syrup so that it runs down the sides of each glass. Then scoop the ice cream to the rim of each glass. For each serving, pour 3 ounces of espresso over the top and press a cookie into the ice cream. Garnish with a drizzle of the cocoa syrup.

MAKES 4 SERVINGS

Mocha Tapioca Affogato

Pichet Ong, P*ONG Dessert Shop & Bar, New York, New York

In New York City, Chinatown and Little Italy are next-door neighbors. With his love for Taiwanese tapioca milk-teas and affogatos from the Italian sidewalk cafes, acclaimed pastry chef Pichet Ong decided to combine the concepts, adding chocolate as a third element. The chocolate ice cream is sweetened with condensed milk, whose marshmallow overtones embellish the mocha assembly. If you have neither Vietnamese coffee nor an ice cream maker, you can revert to the traditional espresso and use store-bought chocolate ice cream, but the tapioca is a must. You can prepare each component—the tapioca, coffee, and ice cream—ahead of time. Room-temperature coffee works fine. If you don't wish to assemble the affogato right away, transfer the drained tapioca pearls to a large container and cover with enough cold water to cover the tapioca by one inch. Refrigerate until ready to use, then drain and serve.

COFFEE

$1/2$ cup Vietnamese chicory or French roast coffee grounds

TAPIOCA

$1/2$ cup sugar

$1/2$ teaspoon salt

6 cups water

$1/2$ cup small tapioca pearls ($1/8$-inch diameter)

CHOCOLATE-CONDENSED MILK ICE CREAM

$2 1/2$ cups whole milk

$3/4$ cups sweetened condensed milk

$1/2$ teaspoon salt

8 ounces Bittersweet Valrhona Chocolate (66 to 72% cacao), chopped

$1/2$ teaspoon vanilla extract

To brew the coffee, use a traditional Vietnamese drip coffee canister, if you have one. Otherwise, use a coffee machine. Line the filter with 2 paper filters and pack the grinds tightly. Add 3 cups of water to the machine and use the slow-drip option, if available. You should end up with about 2 cups of very strong coffee.

To make the tapioca, combine the sugar, salt, and 6 cups of water in a large saucepan and bring to a boil over high heat. Add the tapioca and cook, stirring continuously, until the water returns to a rapid boil. Lower the heat to medium and continue stirring, 15 minutes, until the tapioca is cooked through. It's done when the tapioca balls are almost translucent with a pinpoint of white in the center. The tapioca balls should be tender but still chewy. Drain the tapioca, rinse under cold running water, drain again, and immediately divide among 8 tall serving glasses.

To make the ice cream, combine the milk, condensed milk, and salt in a medium saucepan and set over medium heat. When bubbles start to form around the edge, about 5 minutes, add the chocolate pieces, whisking constantly, until completely melted. Strain the mixture into a bowl that has been placed over ice water and stir until the mixture is cold throughout. Add the vanilla extract. Transfer the mixture to your ice cream maker and follow manufacturer's instructions. After churning, freeze for a firm ice cream or enjoy immediately.

MAKES 1^1/$_2$ PINTS

Place 2 scoops of ice cream in each of the 8 tapioca glasses and divide the hot coffee among the servings. Serve immediately with a fat straw or spoon.

MAKES 8 SERVINGS

Buzz Cupcakes

Sue McCown, Coco La Ti Da, Seattle, Washington

Sue McCown made her mark with whimsical artistry in the City of Coffee, with stints at Campagne, the Painted Table, Obachine, and Earth & Ocean, before embarking on her own ambitious venture, a dessert lounge call Coco La Ti Da. One of her signature desserts suggests a miniature wedding cake and celebrates the marriage of coffee and chocolate. Seattle's "Diva of Desserts" appeals to our collective childhood memories with these devil's-food cupcakes. Her special twist is to bake them with espresso and cocoa and frost them with a Kahlua-white chocolate ganache. (She leaves the frosting-to-cake ratio up to you.)

DEVIL'S FOOD CAKE

1/2 cup plus 2 tablespoons butter, softened

2 cups sugar

2 eggs

2 cups all-purpose flour

6 tablespoons unsweetened cocoa powder

1 teaspoon baking powder

2 teaspoons vanilla extract

1 cup espresso or very strong coffee, cold

FROSTING

2 tablespoons instant espresso

1/2 cup milk

1/2 cup butter

4 ounces white chocolate, chopped

1 teaspoon coffee liqueur

2 1/2 cups confectioners' sugar

Preheat oven to 350°F. Butter and dust with flour cupcake pans for 24 cupcakes. Using an electric mixer, cream the butter and sugar on medium speed until creamy, approximately 5 minutes. Add the eggs, one at a time, beating well between each addition. Add the flour, cocoa powder, baking powder, and vanilla extract and mix well. Then add the coffee and

CONTINUED

mix well. Divide batter into the cupcake pans; a 2-inch ice cream scoop works great for this. Bake for about 25 to 30 minutes minutes until a toothpick comes out clean. Cool slightly in the pan, then transfer to a rack to cool completely before frosting.

To make the frosting, mix instant espresso with the milk, and let stand until espresso is dissolved. In a double boiler, melt the butter and white chocolate together, beat until smooth, then add the coffee liqueur. Beat in 1 cup of the confectioners' sugar. Add half the milk mixture, then 1 cup of the confectioners' sugar. Add the remaining half of the milk mixture, then the final $1/2$ cup of confectioners' sugar.

To assemble the cupcakes, pipe the frosting onto the cupcakes.

MAKES 24 CUPCAKES

Sicilian-born Pasqua Rosee opened London's first coffee house in Cornhill in 1652; in 1657, London's first chocolate house was opened by a Frenchman, whose name has been lost to history.

Chocolate Terrine with Coffee Sabayon

Michelle Garbee, Bastille, Alexandria, Virginia

For this splendid dessert, Michelle Garbee, a former Watergate Hotel executive pastry chef, chooses Valrhona Manjari, a dark bittersweet chocolate, that blends Criollos and Trinitaros cocoa beans from South America. "The intense hints of red fruits in the Valrhona Manjari strike a wonderful balance with the earthy bitterness of the espresso," explains Michelle, "and each component seems to perfectly balance the other." The finishing touch, a rich but not overwhelming espresso sabayon spooned over each portion, elevates the dish to refined sophistication.

CHOCOLATE TERRINE

16 ounces Manjari Valrhona Bittersweet Chocolate (64% cacao)

2 ounces unsweetened chocolate

2/3 cup espresso or very strong coffee

2/3 cup Kahlua or coffee liqueur

3 egg yolks

6 egg whites

1/4 teaspoon salt

1 teaspoon vanilla extract

1/4 cup granulated sugar

3/4 cup heavy cream, cold

SABAYON

4 egg yolks

1/4 cup sugar

1 1/2 ounces Kahlua or coffee liquor

1/4 cup heavy cream, whipped to soft peaks

1/2 teaspoons ground espresso

To make the terrine, line a small loaf pan with plastic wrap, covering the bottom and all sides. In a heat-proof bowl, combine the chocolate, espresso, and Kahlua. Place the bowl over a pan of gently simmering water. Gently stir until the chocolate has completely melted. Whisk in the egg yolks and remove from heat.

CONTINUED

In a separate bowl, combine the egg whites, salt, vanilla extract, and granulated sugar and whip until glossy stiff peaks form. Fold a quarter of the meringue into the chocolate mixture. When fully combined, add the remaining meringue and fold until completely incorporated.

Whip the cold heavy cream until it forms soft peaks and fold into the chocolate mixture. Pour the finished chocolate mixture into the loaf pan and gently tap down to release any air pockets that may be trapped inside. Smooth the top of the chocolate and place in the refrigerator. Allow to set at least 4 hours or until firm. The terrine can be made a couple of days in advance. Just wrap with extra plastic wrap to seal the top of the loaf pan and keep refrigerated until ready to use.

To make the sabayon, combine the yolks, sugar, and Kahlua in a heat-proof bowl and whisk until thoroughly combined. Place the bowl over a pan of gently simmering water and continue whisking until the mixture becomes thick and glossy, about 4 minutes. It should hold its shape when spooned onto a plate.

Transfer the mixture to a clean bowl and place it in a larger bowl of ice water and whisk until the mixture feels cold. Fold in the whipped heavy cream and ground espresso. Cover and chill for up to 4 hours before serving.

MAKES 6 TO 8 SERVINGS

Mocha & Cocoa Nib Tiramisu Parfait

Mindy Segal, HOTCHOCOLATE, Chicago, Illinois

Legend has it that tiramisu, the Italian layered *semifreddo,* was invented in a restaurant called *Le Beccherie* in Treviso, near Venice. The women who worked in a nearby brothel would drop in for the dessert as a *tirami-su* or "pick-me-up" between customers. The traditional tiramisu is transformed into a postmodern parfait by Mindy Segal who refined her craft in the pastry kitchens of Spago, mk, and Charlie Trotter's before launching HOTCHOCOLATE. Note: Cocoa nibs are roasted cocoa beans that have been separated from their husks and broken into small bits. Although not always easy to find, they are worth the effort. Check the Resources on page 128.

MOCHA MOUSSE

9 ounces milk chocolate

1/4 cup brewed espresso

1 1/2 cups heavy cream

COCOA NIB TIRAMISU

1 cup cocoa nibs

2 cups heavy cream

1/4 cup granulated sugar

1 cup mascarpone softened

1 tablespoon espresso granules

1 teaspoon Kahlua

CHOCOLATE WAFERS

1 small block milk chocolate, shaved for garnish

To make the mocha mousse, melt the milk chocolate over a double boiler. In a separate bowl, combine the warm espresso and melted milk chocolate, stirring until smooth. Set aside.

CONTINUED

Whip the cream until it forms medium peaks, then fold into the chocolate. Set aside.

To make the cocoa nib tiramisu, combine the cocoa nibs and heavy cream. Cover, and refrigerate overnight. The following day, strain the cocoa nibs from the heavy cream and discard the nibs. Whip the heavy cream and sugar until it reaches medium stiffness. Add the mascarpone. Whip on high speed until the mixture is stiff. Add the espresso granules and set aside.

To assemble, crush the chocolate wafers into crumbs. Fill 6 wine goblets half way with the mocha mousse. Cover with the crushed wafers. Fill the rest of each glass with the cocoa nib tiramisu, then cover the top of each serving with chocolate shavings.

MAKES 6 SERVINGS

According to Harvard Medical School researchers, coffee may reduce the risk of developing gallstones, discourage the development of colon cancer, improve cognitive function, and reduce the risk of diabetes, liver damage, and Parkinson's disease. Coffee has also been shown to improve performance in long-duration physical activities.

Chocolate-Espresso-Walnut Brownies

Lee Posey, Pearl Bakery, Portland, Oregon

Influences collected from extensive travels in Italy have inspired and guided Lee Posey's artisan baking. She feels that the success of any chocolate-coffee combination depends on the quality and freshness of the espresso. At the bakery, Lee and her crew have the luxury of brewing high-quality espresso and using it immediately upon extraction, providing an aggressive coffee flavor that is especially effective in the brownies. If you don't have a countertop espresso machine at home, you can use instant espresso powder. Better still, run out to get freshly-pulled shots from your nearest coffee bar.

4 ounces all-purpose flour

1 ounce cocoa powder

1/2 teaspoon baking powder

6 ounces bittersweet chocolate (60% cacao)

6 tablespoons unsalted butter

2 large eggs

1/2 teaspoon kosher salt

1 teaspoon vanilla extract

8 ounces granulated sugar

1/3 cup freshly brewed espresso, warm

4 ounces walnuts, toasted

Preheat oven to 375°F. Butter an 8-inch square cake pan and line the bottom and two sides with a piece of foil. The foil should come just above the edge of the pan. Butter the foil.

In a small bowl, combine the flour, cocoa powder, and baking powder and set aside. Melt the chocolate and butter together in a bowl over a double boiler or in a microwave. Set aside to cool slightly. In a separate bowl, whisk the eggs, salt, and vanilla together. Add the sugar in a slow stream and continue whisking until the sugar is dissolved into the egg mixture. Whisk in the espresso and then the melted chocolate/butter.

CONTINUED

Chocolate-Espresso-Walnut Brownies, *continued*

Stir in the flour mixture with a rubber spatula, and finally, stir in the walnuts. Pour the batter evenly into the prepared pan and bake for about 25 minutes. The brownies should still be a little soft in the center. Let cool completely. Loosen the brownies from the pan by tugging gently at the foil overhang. Lift out by the foil handles and transfer it to a cutting board. These brownies are tricky to cut neatly while still warm from the oven. They are much easier to cut if they've been refrigerated for an hour or so. Use a very sharp knife that has been heated under hot running water.

MAKES 10 TO 12 SERVINGS

In *Bacchus in Tuscany*, published in 1685, Francesco Redi extolled the greatness of chocolate and coffee with inspired verses.

Bittersweet Chocolate-Coffee-Toffee Bread Pudding

Hedy Goldsmith, Nemo, Shoji Sushi, Big Pink, Miami Beach, Florida

Creatively matching distinctive flavors is the signature style that Hedy Goldsmith brings to the pastry kitchens of three Miami Beach restaurants, and at each of these very different eateries, desserts flawlessly suit the mood. Her inspiration for pairing chocolate with coffee is a tradition-breaking brioche bread pudding. This New England favorite has a whimsical, Gold Coast twist. Serve it warm from the oven with your favorite ice cream, drizzled liberally with espresso caramel sauce.

PUDDING

1 1/2 cups heavy cream

1/3 cup half-and-half

1 vanilla bean, split lengthwise

Pinch of kosher salt

1 cup whole dark roasted coffee beans

6 egg yolks

3 tablespoons sugar

5 ounces high-quality bittersweet chocolate, chopped

6 cups day-old brioche cubes, crusts removed

2 tablespoons finely ground espresso powder

1/2 cup crushed Heath Bar

ESPRESSO-CARAMEL SAUCE

2 1/4 cups sugar

3/4 cups water

1/2 cup espresso liquid, room temperature

1 cup heavy cream

1 tablespoon vanilla extract

Preheat oven to 325°F. Butter the inside of a 1.5-quart soufflé dish. In a small saucepan, bring the cream, half-and-half, vanilla bean, salt, and espresso beans to a simmer. Remove from heat and let steep, covered, for 20 minutes. Strain and set aside. In a medium bowl, whisk together the egg yolks and sugar. Gradually whisk some of the hot cream into the yolk mixture, then add the remaining cream, whisking constantly. Add the finely chopped chocolate and espresso powder and continue to whisk until the chocolate melts. Add the bread cubes and stir until they are evenly soaked. Place the dish in a baking pan and place on the middle rack of the oven. Pour enough hot water into the pan so that about I inch of the dish is sitting in water. Bake for 45 minutes. Check the water level and add more, if needed, to keep constant. Insert a knife into the pudding. It should come out clean. Remove from the oven and let stand 20 minutes. Invert onto a serving platter.

To make the espresso-caramel sauce, in a heavy saucepan, stir the sugar and water together. Cook over medium heat until all the sugar is dissolved. Increase the heat and continue cooking until the mixture is golden brown in color. Remove from the heat and slowly add the espresso, stirring carefully and continuously. Add the cream and vanilla extract. Sprinkle with the crushed Heath Bar. Serve warm. The sauce can be made a day in advance and reheated over a double boiler.

MAKES 2¹/₄ CUPS

To serve, scoop the warm bread pudding onto individual serving plates, drizzle with the warm sauce, and enjoy immediately.

MAKES 4 TO 6 SERVINGS

Chocolate-Espresso Luxury Cake

Nicole Coady, Finale Desserterie, Cambridge, Massachusetts

Pastry chef Nicole Coady "takes the cake" with a deep, dark, flourless indulgence that weds Guanaja chocolate to rich espresso. The most powerfully flavored of the Valrhona Grands Crus, Guanaja is a blend of Criollos and Trinitaros cocoa beans from South America. Its intense bittersweetness, strong bouquet, and notes of molasses and burnt-coffee provide contrast to a spicy, chocolatey, full-bodied Italian espresso. Nicole suggests a dab of whipped cream or a scoop of vanilla gelato as accompaniment. The cake can also be made in smaller ramekins to be enjoyed warm straight from the oven.

2 1/2 sticks butter, unsalted

8 ounces Valrhona Guanaja Chocolate

3 ounces unsweetened chocolate

4 eggs

5 ounces espresso, strong coffee can be substituted

3/4 cup sugar

1/4 stick butter, to grease pan

Boiling water

Preheat oven to 300°F. Melt the butter over low heat in a small sauce pan. Do not allow the butter to brown. Melt the chocolate in a bowl over a double boiler or in a microwave at 120°F, stirring frequently. While the chocolate is melting, beat the eggs slightly. Brew the espresso. Combine the hot butter and sugar in a mixing bowl until fully incorporated. Add the melted chocolate and continue to mix. Slowly add the slightly beaten eggs and continue to mix. Add the hot coffee and continue to stir until the mixture is smooth and shiny.

Brush the melted butter into an 8 × 3-inch springform cake pan to lightly grease, then wrap outside of pan with aluminum foil to create a waterproof seal. Place the cake pan inside a 2-inch deep roasting pan and then pour the cake batter into the cake pan. Place the pans on the middle rack of the oven, then pour enough boiling water into the roasting pan so that the cake pan is sitting in about 1 inch of water.

Bake 60 to 70 minutes. Cake will feel slightly firm when done. Be very careful when removing from the oven, as the water will be very hot. Remove the cake pan from the roasting pan. Allow the cake to cool completely, then refrigerate to set. Once set, carefully remove the cake from the springform pan and transfer to a serving plate. Allow the cake to warm up to room temperature before serving.

MAKES 10 TO 12 SERVINGS

Mocha Sabayon with Spiked Figs

Nathan Miller, The Kitchen Café, Boulder, Colorado

The Italian sweet tooth originated in Venice, where cane sugar, as well as coffee and chocolate, were first imported from Africa. Sweet, foamy sabayon, or *zabaglione,* was developed by the Venetians as a dessert accompaniment to fruit, especially their beloved figs. (Caravaggio paid homage to the fig in no less than five of his masterpieces.) Borrowing selectively from culinary history and his own creative instincts, pastry chef Nathan Miller adorns the brandy-spiked figs with a delectably lush mantle of mocha sabayon—a stylish conclusion to a special dinner party.

SPIKED FIGS

30 dried figs

1 cup brandy

1 cup apple cider

1/2 cup sugar

Pinch of salt

1 orange, unpeeled and sliced

1 cinnamon stick

SABAYON

1/2 cup heavy cream, whipped

6 egg yolks

1/3 cup sugar

3 tablespoons cocoa powder

1 cup strong coffee, warm

To make the figs, trim the stems from the dried figs and cut each fig in half. Place them in a saucepan and add the brandy, apple cider, sugar, and salt, then stir. Cover the mixture with cheesecloth. Place the sliced orange and cinnamon stick on top of cheesecloth. Bring the liquid to a boil, then reduce the heat to a slow simmer. Cook over low heat until the liquid reduces by about a third. Remove the cheesecloth. The figs may be served warm or cold.

To make the sabayon, heat the water for the double boiler. Whip the heavy cream until it forms stiff peaks. Set aside in the refrigerator until you are ready use it. In the top of the double boiler, combine the egg yolks, sugar, and cocoa powder, stirring continuously until incorporated. Slowly pour the warm coffee into the egg yolk mixture while whisking briskly. Continue whisking the liquid until it becomes thick and ribbon-like. Let the sabayon chill in the refrigerator; when cool, fold in the stiff whipped cream.

To serve, pour a little sabayon onto individual serving plates, arrange the figs on the plates, and pour the remaining sabayon over the fruit.

MAKES 6 SERVINGS

You're a deep thinker and like the buzz of discussion and debate. After all, this is why coffee and chocolate houses came into being.

MURRAY LANGHAM,
CHOCOLATE THERAPY

PB & J Mocha

Vera Tong, Compass, New York, New York

At Compass, pastry chef Vera Tong creates a range of desserts with an equal measure of imagination and playfulness. She turns tradition on its head by putting a modern, grown-up twist on an American childhood classic. The warm white chocolate-coffee liquid is served in a wide-mouth cocktail glass. Beside it sits a bowl containing a scoop of sorbet, and a moment before it is served, the sorbet is dropped into the mocha, creating an icy-hot concoction, then playfully garnished with crunchy peanut-butter balls.

HOT MOCHA

2 cups half-and-half

1 tablespoon green cardamom pods

2 tablespoons 100% arabica coffee

1¹/₂ cups finely chopped Belcolate White Chocolate

CONCORD GRAPE SORBET

1 pound concord grapes, stems removed

4 tablespoons sugar

¹/₂ cup simple syrup (see Caffé Shakerato con Cioccolato, page 40, for recipe)

¹/₂ teaspoon citric acid

¹/₄ cup water

FRIED PEANUT-BUTTER BALLS

1 cup smooth peanut butter

¹/₄ teaspoon salt

¹/₂ cup confectioners' sugar

1¹/₂ cups panko breadcrumbs

1 teaspoon Ceylon cinnamon

1 egg

1 cup flour

To make the mocha, scald half-and-half with the cardamom and coffee beans and cover with aluminum foil. Remove from heat and allow to steep for 1 hour. Reheat the mixture until it boils, then strain. Add the white chocolate pieces and mix until they are completely dissolved.

To make the sorbet, in a medium saucepan, combine the grapes and sugar and bring to a boil. Let cool. Transfer to a food processor and pulse. Do not break up the seeds or the sorbet will have an undesired peppery flavor. Chill the mixture overnight and strain through a fine sieve. Add the simple syrup, citric acid, and water, and combine using an immersion blender. Chill the mixture for at least 4 hours before freezing in an ice cream maker. (Be sure to follow the manufacturers instructions.)

To make the fried peanut butter balls, in a stand mixer, combine the peanut butter, salt, and sugar and mix until smooth. Chill the mixture in the refrigerator until firm. Form 1-inch balls (about the size of a gumball). Combine the panko breadcrumbs and cinnamon in a bowl. In a separate bowl, lightly beat the egg and set aside. Place the flour in a third bowl. Dredge each peanut butter ball in the flour, then coat with the egg, and roll in the breadcrumbs. Preheat a fryer to 350°F. Fry the peanut butter balls until golden brown, about 2 minutes.

To serve, fill six 10-ounce cocktail glasses halfway with the hot mocha. Place a scoop of sorbet into each glass, and garnish with peanut butter balls.

MAKES 6 SERVINGS

Eskimocha

Deborah Racicot, Gotham Bar and Grill, New York, New York

In the early stages of her remarkable career, Deborah Racicot supplied creative desserts to some of Seattle's best coffee bars. Today, as pastry chef at one of New York's great restaurants, she continues to find inspiration in the partnership of chocolate and coffee, "my two favorite flavors," says Deborah. "In a city that loves innovation and surprise, desserts go in and out of style," she explains, "but some version of the mocha combination always survives." Her version of frozen mochaccino was developed as a component in an elaborate parfait she created at Gotham Bar and Grill. On its own, the light, iced mousse becomes an easy-to-make party dessert.

7 egg yolks

1 cup sugar

2 cups milk

1/4 cup instant espresso

4 ounces milk chocolate (such as Valrhona Jivara Lactee), finely chopped

2 1/2 cups heavy cream

Pinch of salt

Cocoa powder, for garnish

In the bowl of a food processor with a whipping attachment, place the yolks with the sugar. Whip on high until thick and ribbony, approximately 5 minutes. In a small saucepan, place the milk and instant espresso. Over medium heat, bring to a simmer. Slowly pour the milk mixture into the egg yolks on low speed. Return the mixture to the saucepan. Place the finely chopped chocolate into the food processor bowl, and set aside. Over low heat, whisk the milk-egg yolk mixture until you see the first sign of a boil. Quickly pour the mixture into the bowl with the chocolate. Combine thoroughly and set aside for 5 minutes to allow the chocolate to melt. Beginning on medium speed, gradually combine the mousse mixture, slowly increasing the speed, until the mixture is room temperature. Set aside.

Place six 8-ounce coffee cups in the freezer.

In a separate food processor bowl, add the 2 cups of heavy cream and whip until it forms medium peaks. Fold the whipped cream into the chocolate mixture and season with the salt. Pour the mousse into the chilled coffee cups and return them to the freezer for up to 8 hours or overnight.

To serve, whip the remaining cream until it forms stiff peaks. Place a dollop of the whipped cream on each frozen mochaccino and dust with cocoa powder.

MAKES 6 EIGHT-OUNCE PORTIONS

Chocolate is a perfect food, as wholesome as it is delicious, a beneficent restorer of exhausted power. It is the best friend of those engaged in literary pursuits.

BARON JUSTUS VON LIEBIG

As soon as coffee is in your stomach, there is a general commotion. Ideas begin to move . . . similies arise, the paper is covered. Coffee is your ally and writing ceases to be a struggle.

HONORÉ DE BALZAC

Moka Pots de Crème

Pascal Janvier, Fleur de Cocoa, Los Gatos, California

He was a pastry apprentice as a young boy in Normandy, France. Master pastry chef and artisan chocolatier Pascal Janvier returns to his roots for a dish of stylish counterpoint and delightful balance. He believes that the interplay of rich chocolate and strong espresso develops a distinctive personality of its own. Traditional pot de crème cups with lids make a wonderful presentation, but other containers can be used such as ramekins, custard cups, or ovenproof coffee or teacups. This silky smooth dessert is perfect for parties because it can be made a few days ahead.

2 cups heavy cream

1 tablespoon instant espresso

4 ounces bittersweet chocolate (60% cacao)

2 1/2 ounces unsweetened chocolate (100% cacao)

6 eggs, separated

4 ounces granulated sugar

Whipped cream

Coffee beans

In a heavy saucepan, combine the heavy cream with the instant espresso and bring to a boil. Pour the boiling cream over the bittersweet chocolate and unsweetened chocolate. While the hot cream is melting the chocolates, in a separate bowl, briskly whisk together the egg yolks and sugar. Add the egg mixture to the chocolate cream mixture and stir to combine. Strain the mixture and divide among 6 six-ounce ramekins.

CONTINUED

In a convection oven, bake at 212°F for 20 minutes or until barely set. Remove the ramekins gently from the oven and place in the refrigerator for 45 minutes.

In a conventional oven, preheat oven to 300°F. In a 9 × 13 × 2-inch roasting pan, place a cloth dishtowel or a double thickness of paper towels in the bottom. Place the ramekins on the towel, making sure they aren't touching each other or the sides of the pan and place the pan in the middle rack of the oven. Pour enough hot water to reach halfway up the sides of the ramekins. Bake for 30 to 35 minutes, or until the sides are set but the centers are still a bit wobbly. Remove from the oven and transfer the ramekins to a rack to cool to room temperature. Then refrigerate to cool completely at least 1 hour.

Decorate with a rosette of whipped cream and the coffee beans. Serve cool but not cold.

MAKES 6 SIX-OUNCE SERVINGS

Resources

CHOCOLATE

Amedei
chocosphere.com

Callebaut
chocosphere.com

Cioccolateria Slitti
chocosphere.com

Domori
chocosphere.com

E. Guittard
chocosphere.com

El Rey
chocosphere.com

Endangered Species
chocolatebar.com

Michel Cluizel
chocosphere.com

Santander
chocosphere.com

Scharffen Berger
scharffenberger.com

Valrhona
chocosphere.com

HOT CHOCOLATE

Browne's Hand Made
Chocolates
brownes.co.uk

Café Tasse
chocosphere.com

Charbonnel et Walker
charbonnel.co.uk

Chocolate Bar
chocolatebarnyc.com

Chocolat Bonnat
chocolatetradingco.com

Chocolat Vitale
cocoaconnoisseur.com

Christopher Elbow
Chocolates
elbowchocolates.com

Cioco Delice
espressotiamao.com

Dagoba Organic Chocolate
dagobachocolate.com

Dolfin
chocosphere.com

Dufflet Pastries
dufflet.com

Enric Rovira
seventypercent.com

Fauchon
fauchon.com

Fran's Chocolates, Ltd.
franschocolates.com

Green & Black's
chocosphere.com

Holy Chocolate
holychocolate.com

Jacques Torres
mrchocolate.com

Kakawa Chocolates
kakawachocolates.com

L. A. Burdick
burdickchocolate.com

La Maison du Chocolat
lamaisonduchocolat.com

Lake Champlain Chocolates
lakechamplainchocolates.com

Les Confitures à l'Ancienne
chocosphere.com

Max Brenner Chocolat
maxbrenner.com

MarieBelle
newyorkfirst.com

Recchiuti
recchiuti.com

Schokinag North America-
drinkyourchocolate.com

Vosges Haut-Chocolat
vosgeschocolate.com

Valor Chocolates
chocosphere.com

Williams-Sonoma
williams-sonoma.com

Xocoatl
chocolatecartel.com

MEXICAN CHOCOLATE

Abuelita
mexgrocer.com

Ibarra
mexgrocer.com

Moctezuma
mexgrocer.com

COCOA POWDER

Bellagio
caffedamore.com

Christopher Elbow
elbowchocolates.com

Domori
chocosphere.com

Droste Nederland
cardullos.com

Fairly Traded Organic Hot
Cocoa Mix
equalexchange.com

Ghirardelli Chocolate
ghirardelli.com

Godiva
godiva.com

Michel Cluizel
chocosphere.com

Mocafe
mocafe.net

Omanhene Cocoa Bean
omahene.com

Serendipity Frozen Hot
Chocolate
newyorkfirst.com

Venchi
chocosphere.com

COCOA NIBS

Valrhona
chocosphere.com

Dagoba
chocosphere.com

Theo
chocosphere.com

COFFEE

Allegro Coffee
allegro-coffee.com

Armeno Coffee
armeno.com

Barefoot Coffee Roasters
barefootcoffeeroasters.com

Caffe Artigiano
caffeartigiano.com

Coffee Klatch Roasting
klatchroasting.com

Doma Coffee Roasting
Company
domacoffee.com

Espresso Vivace
espressovivace.com

Gimme Coffee
gimmecoffee.com

Giuliano Caffé
chocosphere.com

Illy Caffé
illyusa.com

Intelligentsia Coffee
intelligentsiacoffee.com

Koa Coffee
koacoffee.com

Peet's Coffee & Tea
peets.com

Starbuck's Coffee
starbucksstore.com

Stumptown Coffee Roasters
stumptowncoffee.com

Thanksgiving Coffee
thanksgivingcoffee.com

Zoka Coffee Roasters
zokacoffee.com

INSTANT ESPRESSO

King Arthur Flour
kingarthurflour.com

Medaglia d'Oro
medagliadoro.com

SYRUPS

Artista
artistagourmet.com

DaVinci
davincigourmet.com

Dolce
stearns-lehman.com

Eclipse
autocrat.com

Fabbri
italiansyrups.com

Lyle's
addflavour.com

Monin
monin.com

Mont Blanc Gourmet
montblancgourmet.com

Morning Glory
morningglorysyrup.com

Torani
torani.com

COFFEE EQUIPMENT

Bodum
newyorkfirst.com

Braun
braun.com

Breville
brevilleusa.com

Capresso
capresso.com

Chef's Catalog
chefscatalog.com

Espresso Zone
espressozone.com

Espresso Parts
espressoparts.com

Fante's Kitchen Ware
fantes.com

Faema
faema.it

Gaggia
gaggia.com

Krups
krups.com

La Pavoni
lapavoni.com

Nuova Simonelli
nuovasimonelliusa.com

Rancilio
rancilio.com

Saeco
saeco-usa.com

Solis
soliscoffee.com

Sweet Maria's
sweetmarias.com

SERVINGWARE

Bicerin goblets
newyorkfirst.com

Tazzina cups/glassware
newyorkfirst.com

Hot drink cups/mugs
newyorkfirst.com

Index

Ghana, chocolate production of, 2
Gianduja chocolate, 16, 56
Godiva Dark Chocolate Liqueur, 78, 79
Godiva White Chocolate Liqueur, 76
Goldsmith, Hedy, 114
Gordon, Clay, 40
Gotham Bar and Grill, 20, 122
Grand Marnier Cordon Rouge, 84
Grand Prix International de la Chocolaterie, 21
grapes, concord, 120
ground espresso powder, 107, 114
guhwah, 45
Guittard Dark Chocolate Syrup, 29, 63
Guittard Sweet Ground Chocolate, 51
Gulf Coast, 47

H

half-and-half, 37, 43, 44, 48, 51, 56, 61, 86, 114, 120
Hanson, Stephen, 70
Happy Rooster, 81
Harvard Medical School, coffee research at, 127
hazelnut foam, 56
hazelnut paste, 24, 56
hazelnuts, 16, 91
Heath Bar, 114
Hines Public Market Coffee, 43

honey, 9, 43, 51, 68. *see also* specific types of honey
Hot Chocolate, 84
hot fudge, 35
Hot Fudge Sauce, 35
Hot Mocha, 120
HOTCHOCOLATE, 109

I

Ibarra chocolate, 66
ibriks, 32
Ice Cream, 99, 100
immune system, chocolate and, 72
ingredients. *see also* specific ingredients
  overview, 5–6
instant espresso, 96, 104, 122, 124
Institute Alberghiero, 17
Italian sodas, 8

J

Jamaican Blue Mountain coffee, 21
Jean-Louis restaurant, 84
Joe (the Art of Coffee), 48
JS Bon Bons, 50

K

Kaffa, Ethiopia, 1
Kaffee Schokolade Coffeecake, 96–98, 97
Kahlua, 104, 109
Kahlua liqueur, 107
Kaplan, Nicole, 56

Kathy Casey Food Studios, 82
Katz, Elizabeth, 70
Kenya, characteristics of coffee from, 2
Kenya highlands, 50
Kenyan coffee beans, 50
The Kitchen Café, 118
Klassen, Seneca, 47
Kleinberg, Neil, 35
Kopi Luwak coffee, 21

L

La Mocha Loca, 37
La Palapa restaurant, 30
La Procope restaurant, 25
Langham, Murray, 119
Latah Bistro, 51
Lava Java Café, 68–69
Le Beccherie Restaurant, 109
lecithin granules, 56
lemongrass, 60, 68
lemongrass-chocolate purée, 68
lemongrass syrup, 68
lemons, 32, 68
liver damage, coffee and, 110
London, England, first coffee house in, 106
Luchetti, Emily, 85
Luu, Tina, 99

M

macchiato, 43
macchina, 63
macinazione, 63